The World and Its People
NEIGHBORHOODS AND COMMUNITIES

Annotated Teacher's Edition

SILVER BURDETT COMPANY

MORRISTOWN, NEW JERSEY

Glenview, Ill. · San Carlos, Calif. · Dallas · Atlanta

NEIGHBORHOODS

SERIES AUTHORS

Val E. Arnsdorf, Professor,
College of Education, University of Delaware, Newark, Delaware

Carolyn S. Brown, Principal,
Robertson Academy School, Nashville, Tennessee

Kenneth S. Cooper, Professor of History, Emeritus,
George Peabody College for Teachers, Vanderbilt University, Nashville, Tennessee

Alvis T. Harthern, Professor of Education,
University of Montevallo, Montevallo, Alabama

Timothy M. Helmus, Middle School Teacher,
Harrison Park Middle School, Grand Rapids, Michigan

Bobbie P. Hyder, Elementary Education Coordinator,
Madison County School System, Huntsville, Alabama

Theodore Kaltsounis, Professor and Chairman of Curriculum and Instruction,
College of Education, University of Washington, Seattle, Washington

Richard H. Loftin, Director of Curriculum and Staff Development,
Aldine Independent School District, Houston, Texas

Norman J.G. Pounds, Former University Professor of Geography,
Indiana University, Bloomington, Indiana

Edgar A. Toppin, Professor of History and Dean of the Graduate School,
Virginia State University, Petersburg, Virginia

PROGRAM CONTRIBUTORS

Paula Allaert, Third Grade Teacher,
St. Therese School, Portland, Oregon
Carol Armour, Third Grade Teacher,
Marie V. Duffy Elementary School, Wharton, New Jersey
Sandra Breman, Fifth Grade Teacher,
Whitney Young Magnet School, Fort Wayne, Indiana
Vivian Brown, Fifth Grade Teacher,
Silver Spur Elementary School, Rancho Palos Verdes, California
Kim Eyler, Former Elementary School Teacher,
Wyckoff, New Jersey
Sharon Gaydon, Sixth Grade Teacher,
Thompson Middle School, Alabaster, Alabama
Janet Glenn, Second Grade Teacher,
Greene School, Greensboro, North Carolina
Viola Gonzalez, Fifth – Sixth Grade Teacher,
Ryan Elementary School, Laredo, Texas
Ellen Gremillion, Third Grade Teacher,
Parkview Elementary School, Baton Rouge, Louisiana
Lucy Hatch, Fifth – Sixth Grade Teacher,
Taylor Elementary School, Abilene, Texas
Judy Hobson, Fourth Grade Teacher,
Elmdale Elementary School, Springdale, Arkansas
Peggy Hogg, Fourth Grade Teacher,
Dartmouth Elementary School, Richardson, Texas
Geoffrey Kashdan, Special Education Teacher,
Hanover Avenue School, Morris Plains, New Jersey
Gloria Lemos, First Grade Teacher,
Emerson Elementary School, Pasco, Washington
William Lentino, Fifth Grade Teacher,
Lloyd Harbor Elementary School, Huntington, New York
Carolyn Lombardo, Third Grade Teacher,
Ferrara Elementary School, East Haven, Connecticut
Mary Lou Martin, Social Studies Resource Teacher, K – 6,
San Diego Unified School District, San Diego, California
Patricia McWey, Second Grade Teacher,
Martin Luther King School, Providence, Rhode Island
Sandra Murphy Mead, Second Grade Teacher,
L.W. West School, Endicott, New York
Ray Ringley, Fifth Grade Teacher,
Powell Valley Primary School, Big Stone Gap, Virginia
Elaine Sisselman, Fourth Grade Teacher,
Biscayne Gardens Elementary School, Miami, Florida
Katharyn Smith, First Grade Teacher,
The Meadows School, College Park, Georgia
Jan Talbot, Sixth Grade Teacher,
Pope Avenue Elementary School, Sacto, California
Patricia Terai, First Grade Teacher,
Woodin Elementary School, Bothell, Washington
William Tucker, Sixth Grade Teacher,
Alanton Elementary School, Virginia Beach, Virginia
Sister Catherine Zajac, S.S.J., Fourth – Sixth Grade Teacher,
St. Agnes School, Dalton, Massachusetts

AND COMMUNITIES

AUTHORS

BOBBIE P. HYDER

Elementary Education Coordinator
Madison County School System
Huntsville, Alabama

CAROLYN S. BROWN

Principal
Robertson Academy School
Nashville, Tennessee

Annotated Teacher's Edition

CONTENTS

PROGRAM RATIONALE

The Silver Burdett social studies program THE WORLD AND ITS PEOPLE was developed to help students understand the world around them and to instill in them the knowledge and skills necessary for responsible citizenship. Built on a solid factual foundation, the program examines the students' world in an ever-widening circle. THE WORLD AND ITS PEOPLE begins with a study of self and family in Grade 1 and expands in Grades 2 through 6 to a study of neighborhood, community, state, region, nation, and world.

Each book in the series reflects the following belief: *Students need to know, to appreciate, and to do.* A grasp of basic facts is essential in gaining an understanding of social studies. To that end, a wealth of materials is provided. Lesson checkups, chapter and unit reviews, and chapter tests ensure the students' understanding of the text material. Opportunities for development of language, reading, and social studies skills are provided throughout the series through vocabulary study, skills development exercises, and other skills-related activities. Parental involvement is encouraged through the use of a letter to parents provided periodically in the Teacher's Editions.

THE WORLD AND ITS PEOPLE involves much more than a passive acceptance of facts. The program involves *doing*. Students work with maps, charts, graphs, tables, and time lines as a vital part of the learning process. Students build models, conduct interviews, hold debates, and take part in a variety of other activities. In short, students are *active participants*.

While facts are emphasized, it is recognized that those facts, to be meaningful, must be utilized. The function of factual knowledge in THE WORLD AND ITS PEOPLE is to enable students to appreciate themselves, the world around them, and their role as citizens of the United States. Students are led to understand some of the important links between them and their families, community, state, region, nation, and world. In doing so, they develop an appreciation of historic and geographic factors and economic and political relationships that have shaped their world. Moreover, students are given specific suggestions for assuming a responsible role—in a capacity commensurate with age and ability—in their community, state, region, nation, and world. THE WORLD AND ITS PEOPLE not only prepares students for the future but also helps them function meaningfully and effectively in the present.

FEATURES OF THE PUPIL'S EDITION

Feature	Description
A Letter to You from the Author	Preceding the first chapter is a letter of introduction from the author(s) to the pupils. The purpose of the letter is to tell the pupils about the book.
Vocabulary	Vocabulary words are underlined when first appearing.
Map Skills	Each book devotes an entire chapter to map skills. The chapter develops the essential map-reading skills in a logical and systematic way. Starting with the most basic skills and simplest maps in Grade 1, the series develops those skills and builds on them at each grade level. In addition, the many maps included in the other chapters of each book provide the means for reinforcing the skills presented in the map chapter. There are 260 maps located throughout the texts of Grades 1 through 6 in THE WORLD AND ITS PEOPLE series.
Chapter Review	At the end of every chapter is a Chapter Review. The Chapter Review has four categories: Key Facts, Vocabulary Quiz, Review Questions, and Activities.
Key Facts	Key Facts or main ideas from the chapter are listed, providing a valuable tool for reviewing the content of the chapter.
Vocabulary Quiz	Items such as true/false, matching, and completion sentences are used to review or to test vocabulary.

FEATURES OF THE PUPIL'S EDITION

Feature	Description
Review Questions	Review Questions cover all lessons in the chapter. The majority of the questions are recall. Some are thinking questions involving comparing and contrasting, interpreting, applying, and generalizing.
Activities	Activities that require little or no teacher direction are given.
Skills Development	A Skills Development section follows the Chapter Review in each book. This section consists of questions and/or activities that develop reading, language arts, and social studies skills. Some reading skills included are understanding and defining words, following directions, understanding sequence, and recalling information. Language arts skills such as letter writing, expressing a point of view, and oral reports are included. Social studies skills included are reading of maps, charts, photographs, and drawings. Scope and sequence charts for map and globe, reading, and language arts skills, as well as scope and sequence charts for reasoning and societal skills begin on page T14.
Picture Word List/ Glossary	The vocabulary (underlined) words appear in the Picture Word List found in the back of the book for Grade 1. The vocabulary (underlined) words appear in the Glossary found in the back of the book for Grade 2.

FEATURES OF THE TEACHER'S EDITION

Feature	Description
Program Content Outline	A listing of the program content for THE WORLD AND ITS PEOPLE is located on pages T10 – T13.
Program Skills Scope and Sequence	Various skills that are introduced and/or developed throughout the program are listed in scope and sequence charts. The categories of skills include the following: Map and Globe Skills, Reading Skills in social studies, Language Arts Skills in social studies, Reasoning Skills, and Societal Skills.
Letter to Parents	For each chapter, a letter to parents is provided in the teacher's lesson plans. The purpose of this letter is to inform parents of what pupils will be learning about in the chapter.
Chapter Theme	The theme of each chapter is stated as a guide for the teacher in the teacher's lesson plans.
Overview	The Overview gives a brief summary of the chapter content.
Bulletin-Board Display(s)	Ideas and directions for one or more bulletin-board displays, appropriate for the chapter, are provided.
Getting Started	Introductory activities or projects relating to the chapter are suggested under the heading Getting Started.
Lesson Goals	The lesson goals are guides of what the pupil can be expected to have learned on completion of the lesson content. A lesson is a plan for developing a block of material in the Pupil's Edition; it does not necessarily refer to one class session. The teacher's lesson plans provide Pupil's Edition page references for each lesson.

FEATURES OF THE TEACHER'S EDITION

Feature	Description
Reading Vocabulary	Unfamiliar social studies words appearing in the Pupil's Edition lesson are underlined when first appearing. A list of these reading vocabulary words for each lesson is provided in the teacher's lesson plans.
Oral Vocabulary	Words to be introduced in the lesson but not appearing in the Pupil's Edition lesson are listed as oral vocabulary words. A list of these words for each lesson is provided in the teacher's lesson plans.
Teaching Suggestions	Suggestions and activities for each lesson are given in the teacher's lesson plans. Descriptive headings provide a guide for the teacher in selecting desired suggestions and activities. Some examples of these descriptive headings are Map Reading, Reading Recall, Discussion, Making a Chart, Community Resources, Creative Writing, and Research Reports. Vocabulary reinforcement is emphasized in many of the activities. A variety of activities are suggested, but it is not expected that every activity be used. Suggested questions and direct discourse for teachers to quote are provided. This symbol ● designates expanded activities that contain suggestions for use with pupils who have difficulty grasping the concepts and/or pupils who need a challenge.
Supplementary Information	Supplementary Information is provided when needed. It may give some historical background, focus on human interest material, or give fun-to-know kinds of information.
Annotations	Questions and information are surprinted on the pupil's page of the Teacher's Edition. Often answers to such questions will be given in parentheses. Annotations include interesting facts, items not easily observable, unusual information, photo comparisons, supplementary information, and photo-reading questions.
Books and Other Media	This section includes materials of general interest to teachers and pupils. Among these materials are books, films, filmstrips, and records.

PROGRAM CONTENT OUTLINE

PROGRAM CONTENT OUTLINE

PROGRAM CONTENT OUTLINE

EUROPE, AFRICA, ASIA, AND AUSTRALIA

PROGRAM CONTENT OUTLINE

MAP AND GLOBE SKILLS

SKILLS	GRADES	1	2	3	4	5	6
Globe		■	■	■	■	■	■
Continents and Oceans		■	■	■	■	■	■
Landform Identification			■	■	■	■	■
Shape Identification		■	■	■	■	■	■
Cardinal Directions		■	■	■	■	■	■
Legend (Key)		■	■	■	■	■	■
Symbols		■	■	■	■	■	■
Color		■	■	■	■	■	■
Political Boundaries		■	■	■	■	■	■
Pictorial		■	■	■	■	■	■
Abstract		■	■	■	■	■	■
Transition from Photo to Map		■	■	■	■	■	■
Comparative Size		■	■	■	■	■	■
Labels		■	■	■	■	■	■
Location		■	■	■	■	■	■
Inset Maps		■	■	■	■	■	■
Picture Maps		■	■	■			
Directional Arrows		■	■	■			
North Pole			■	■	■	■	■
South Pole			■	■	■	■	■
Floor Plan			■	■		■	■
Thematic Maps				■	■	■	■
Atlas				■	■	■	■
Intermediate Directions				■	■	■	■
Compass Rose				■	■	■	■
Latitude				■	■	■	■
Equator				■	■	■	■
Arctic Circle				■	■	■	■
Antarctic Circle				■	■	■	■

MAP AND GLOBE SKILLS

SKILLS	GRADES	1	2	3	4	5	6
Latitude (continued)							
Tropic of Cancer				■	■	■	■
Tropic of Capricorn				■	■	■	■
Longitude				■	■	■	■
Prime Meridian				■	■	■	■
Using a Coordinate System				■	■	■	■
Hemispheres				■	■	■	■
Shaded Relief				■	■	■	■
Scale				■	■	■	■
Elevation Tints					■	■	■
Mileage Chart				■		■	
Subway Map				■			
Railroad Map						■	
Physical-Political Map					■	■	■
Road Map					■		
Isolines (e.g., contour lines)					■	■	
Profile Maps					■	■	■
Travel Routes						■	■
Historical Maps						■	■
Weather Map							■
Time Zones							■
Projections							■
Diagrams				■	■	■	■
Graphs							
Pictograph		■		■	■		■
Pie Graph			■	■	■		■
Bar Graph			■	■	■	■	■
Line Graph				■	■	■	■
Climograph						■	■

READING SKILLS

SKILLS	GRADES	1	2	3	4	5	6
VOCABULARY BUILDING							
Understanding and defining words by:							
Using objects		■	■	■	■	■	■
Using illustrations		■	■	■	■	■	■
Using a glossary		■	■	■	■	■	■
Using a dictionary				■	■	■	■
Using context clues				■	■	■	■
Alphabetical Order		■	■	■	■	■	■
Synonyms/Antonyms		■	■	■	■	■	■
Prefix/Suffix				■	■	■	■
Acronyms/Abbreviations				■	■	■	■
Word Origins				■	■	■	■
DEVELOPING READING COMPREHENSION							
Understanding and identifying the main idea		■	■	■	■	■	■
Following directions		■	■	■	■	■	■
Understanding relationships		■	■	■	■	■	■
Understanding sequence		■	■	■	■	■	■
Understanding cause and effect		■	■	■	■	■	■
Recalling information		■	■	■	■	■	■
Recognizing attitudes and emotions		■	■	■	■	■	■
Understanding different literary forms		■	■	■	■	■	■
Understanding that facts support main idea			■	■	■	■	■

READING SKILLS

SKILLS	GRADES	1	2	3	4	5	6
DEVELOPING READING COMPREHENSION (continued)							
Identifying purpose for reading			■	■	■	■	■
Reading schedules and calendars			■	■	■	■	■
Identifying topic sentence				■	■	■	■
Distinguishing between the main idea and details				■	■	■	■
Skimming				■	■	■	■
Distinguishing between fact and opinion				■	■	■	■
Summarizing				■	■	■	■
Reading mileage charts				■	■	■	
Reading and interpreting facts from tables				■	■	■	■
Using details to support main idea					■	■	■
Distinguishing between relevant and irrelevant data						■	■
Paraphrasing						■	■
Recognizing and identifying author's or speaker's purpose						■	■
Understanding primary and secondary sources						■	■
Recognizing propaganda						■	■

LANGUAGE ARTS SKILLS

SKILLS	GRADES	1	2	3	4	5	6
Writing Skills ✓							
Letter Writing (personal) ✓		■	■	■	■	■	■
Descriptive Writing ✓			■	■	■	■	■
Narrative Writing ✓			■	■	■	■	■
Report Writing ✓			■	■	■	■	■
Letter Writing (business) ✓			■	■	■	■	■
Book Reports				■	■	■	■
Writing a Diary				■	■	■	■
Outlining				■	■	■	■
Persuasive Writing					■	■	■
SPEAKING SKILLS							
Expressing a Point of View ✓		■	■	■	■	■	■
Oral Reports ✓			■	■	■	■	■
Debate						■	■
LIBRARY SKILLS							
Choosing References				■	■	■	■
Card Catalog				■	■	■	■
Encyclopedia				■	■	■	■
Newspapers and Magazines				■	■	■	■
Vertical File					■	■	■
Readers' Guide to Periodical Literature						■	■
Almanac						■	■

REASONING SKILLS

SKILLS	GRADES	1	2	3	4	5	6
Identifying and expressing preferences and opinions		■	■	■	■	■	■
Generalizing		■	■	■	■	■	■
Making inferences		■	■	■	■	■	■
Drawing conclusions		■	■	■	■	■	■
Comparing and contrasting		■	■	■	■	■	■
Classifying		■	■	■	■	■	■
Interpreting cause and effect			■	■	■	■	■
Gathering information							
Observing		■	■	■	■	■	■
Interviewing			■	■	■	■	■
Using primary sources				■	■	■	■
Using secondary sources				■	■	■	■
Polling						■	■
Identifying a problem				■	■	■	■
Identifying alternatives				■	■	■	■
Recognizing and identifying points of view					■	■	■
Defending a point of view					■	■	■
Predicting						■	■
Developing objectivity						■	■
Making or withholding judgment					■	■	■
Evaluating relevance of information						■	■

SOCIETAL SKILLS

SKILLS	GRADES	1	2	3	4	5	6
LIFE SKILLS							
Telling time		■	■				
Reading a calendar		■	■				
Practicing pedestrian and bicycle safety		■	■				
Reading traffic signs		■	■	■			
Recognizing warning signs and symbols		■	■	■			
Knowing full name and address		■	■	■			
Understanding the importance of good nutrition		■	■	■			
Knowing fire drill procedure		■	■	■			
Knowing when and how to call fire or police help		■	■	■			
Practicing basic safety techniques in home and school		■	■	■			
Knowing emergency telephone numbers		■	■	■			
Using a telephone		■	■	■	■	■	■
Becoming aware of job opportunities		■	■	■	■	■	■
Budgeting and banking		■	■	■	■	■	■
Addressing an envelope			■	■	■	■	■
Using a telephone directory				■	■	■	■
Reading a schedule				■	■	■	■
Filling out forms and applications				■	■	■	■
Reading newspaper ads						■	■
HUMAN RELATIONS							
Developing personal friendships		■	■				
Developing respect for self		■	■	■	■	■	■
Developing respect for others		■	■	■	■	■	■
Working in groups		■	■	■	■	■	■
Recognizing interdependence among people		■	■	■	■	■	■

SOCIETAL SKILLS

SKILLS	GRADES	1	2	3	4	5	6
HUMAN RELATIONS (continued)							
Understanding the importance of courtesy		■	■	■	■	■	
Recognizing other points of view				■	■	■	■
CITIZENSHIP AND VALUES							
Respecting our American heritage and beliefs		■	■	■	■	■	■
Understanding the democratic process		■	■	■	■	■	■
Understanding the role of the citizen in a democracy		■	■	■	■	■	■
Understanding and accepting the need for laws		■	■	■	■	■	■
Developing a respect for rules and laws		■	■	■	■	■	■
Appreciating ethnic heritage		■	■	■	■	■	■
Appreciating such basic values as honesty, equality, loyalty, dependability, cooperation, fair play, and human dignity		■	■	■	■	■	■
Appreciating the dignity in all occupations		■	■	■	■	■	■
Developing pride in one's own work		■	■	■	■	■	■
Developing good work and job habits, e.g., punctuality, neatness, dependability		■	■	■	■	■	■
Understanding the importance of responsibility		■	■	■	■	■	■
Participating in decision making		■	■	■	■	■	■
Understanding the importance of leisure time					■	■	
Respecting the rights of others while exercising one's own						■	■
Recognizing that responsibility and freedom are closely related						■	■
Recognizing and avoiding negative stereotypes						■	■

BOOKS AND OTHER MEDIA

CHAPTER ONE
BOOKS FOR PUPILS

Big Sister, Little Brother. Terry Berger. Milwaukee, Wis.: Raintree Pubs., Inc.

Blackboard Bear. Martha Alexander. New York: The Dial Press.

Do You Know What? Ruth Jayne. Los Angeles: Bowmar/Noble Pubs., Inc.

The Growing Story. Ruth Krauss. New York: Harper & Row, Pubs., Inc.

The Hating Book. Charlotte Zolotow. New York: Harper & Row, Pubs., Inc.

I Can Do It By Myself. Lessie J. Little and Eloise Greenfield. New York: Thomas Y. Crowell Co., Pubs.

Let's Find Out About Names. Valerie Pitt. New York: Franklin Watts, Inc.

Little Brother, No More. Robert Benton. New York: Alfred A. Knopf, Inc.

Little Indian. Peggy Parish. New York: Simon & Schuster, Inc.

Love Is a Special Way of Feeling. Joan Walsh Anglund. New York: Harcourt Brace Jovanovich, Inc.

Someone New. Charlotte Zolotow. New York: Harper & Row, Pubs., Inc.

Sometimes I Worry. Alan Gross. Chicago: Childrens Press.

To Hilda for Helping. Margot Zemach. New York: Farrar, Straus & Giroux, Inc.

Two Can Toucan. David McKee. New York: Harper & Row, Pubs., Inc.

What Color Am I? Loyal Nye. Nashville, Tenn.: Abingdon Press.

Where the Wild Things Are. Maurice Sendak. New York: Harper & Row, Pubs., Inc.

You're a Scared-Cat. Mercer Mayer. New York: Parents' Magazine Press.

BOOKS FOR TEACHERS

All Together: A Child's Treasury of Verse. Dorothy Aldis. New York: G.P. Putnam's Sons.

General Armory of England, Scotland, Ireland and Wales. John B. Burke. Baltimore, Md.: Genealogical Pub. Co., Inc.

The New Age Baby Name Book. Sue Browder. New York: Warner Books, Inc.

OTHER MEDIA
Filmstrips

First Thing: Guess Who's in a Group. New York: Guidance Associates. 141 frames, record or cassette, color.

Importance of You. Santa Monica, Calif.: BFA Educational Media. Set of 4, 32 – 46 frames.

Songstories—I Am Special. Chicago: Encyclopaedia Britannica Educational Corp. Set of 4, 65 frames.

Straight Hair, Curly Hair. Augusta Goldin. New York: Thomas Y. Crowell Co., Pubs. 35 frames, color.

Who Am I? Universal City, Calif.: Universal Education and Visual Arts. Set of 6, 28 – 40 frames.

Films (16mm)

I Am Freedom's Child. Studio City, Calif.: Filmfair Communications. 5 min, optical sound, color.

The Most Important Person: Creative Expression; Feelings; Getting Along with Others. Chicago: Encyclopaedia Britannica Educational Corp. 3 sets of 3 – 6 each, 4 min.

Records

"Free to Be . . . You and Me." Marlo Thomas. *Free to Be . . . You and Me.* New York: McGraw-Hill, Inc.

"It's Me!" *Silver Burdett Music 1*, Record 2.

CHAPTER TWO
BOOKS FOR PUPILS

All Kinds of Families. Norma Simon. Chicago: Albert Whitman & Co.

Are You My Mother? Philip D. Eastman. New York: Beginner Books.

Ask Mister Bear. Marjorie Flack. New York: Macmillan, Inc.

Benjie on His Own. Joan Lexau. New York: The Dial Press.

Birthday. John Steptoe. New York: Holt, Rinehart & Winston, Inc.

Birthday Car. Margaret Hillert. Chicago: Follett Pub. Co.

The Birthday Party. Ruth Krauss. New York: Harper & Row, Pubs., Inc.

Daddies—What They Do all Day. Helen Puner. New York: Lothrop, Lee & Shepard Books.

A Father Like That. Charlotte Zolotow. New York: Harper & Row, Pubs., Inc.

Martin's Father, 2nd ed. Margrit Eichler. Chapel Hill, N.C.: Lollipop Power, Inc.

Mommies at Work. Eve Merriam. New York: Scholastic Book Services.

Neighborhood Knight. Eleanor Schick. New York: Greenwillow Books.

Nine Days to Christmas. Marie H. Ets and Aurora Labastida. New York: The Viking Press.

No Fighting, No Biting. Else H. Minarik. New York: Harper & Row, Pubs., Inc.

Nobody Asked Me If I Wanted a Baby Sister. Martha Alexander. New York: The Dial Press.

Noel for Jeanne-Marie. Francoise. New York: Charles Scribner's Sons.

Oh Lord, I Wish I Was a Buzzard. Polly Greenberg. New York: Macmillan, Inc.

Six Silver Spoons. Robert Quackenbush. New York: Harper & Row, Pubs., Inc.

Striped Ice Cream. Joan M. Lexau. Philadelphia: J.B. Lippincott Co.

Where Are the Mothers? Dorothy Marino. Philadelphia: J.B. Lippincott Co.

BOOKS FOR TEACHERS

The Complete Book of Hanukkah. Kinneret Chiel. New York: Ktav Pub. House, Inc.

Hanukkah. Norma Simon. New York: Thomas Y. Crowell Co., Pubs.

Happy Days. Christine Price. New York: U.S. Committee for UNICEF.

Indian Festivals. Paul Showers. New York: Thomas Y. Crowell Co., Pubs.

OTHER MEDIA
Filmstrips

Five Families. New York: Scholastic Magazines, Inc. Set of 5, 66 frames.

Robert and His Family. Chicago: Society for Visual Education, Inc. Set of 4, 34 – 43 frames.

Six Families in the U.S. Chicago: Encyclopaedia Britannica Education Corp. Set of 6, 45 frames.

Understanding Changes in the Family, Parts 1 – 5. New York: Guidance Associates. 50 – 73 frames, record or cassette, color.

Films (16 mm)

Families Are Different and Alike. Chicago: Coronet Instructional Films. 11 min, color or b/w.

The Most Important Person: Identity. Chicago: Encyclopaedia Britannica Educational Corp. Set of 6, 4 min.

Records

"Grandma's Birthday." *Silver Burdett Music 1*, Record 8.

CHAPTER THREE
BOOKS FOR PUPILS

Blueberries for Sal. Robert McCloskey. New York: The Viking Press.

Bread and Jam for Frances. Russell Hoban. New York: Harper & Row, Pubs., Inc.

Fresh Cider and Pie. Franz Brandenberg. New York: Macmillan, Inc.

Green Eggs and Ham. Dr. Seuss. New York: Beginner Books.

Hamburgers, and Ice Cream for Dessert. Eleanor Clymer. New York: E.P. Dutton Pub. Co., Inc.

Johnny Cake. Joseph Jacobs. New York: G.P. Putnam's Sons.

Let's Find Out About Thanksgiving. Charles Shapp and Martha Shapp. New York: Franklin Watts, Inc.

More Potatoes! Millicent R. Selsam. New York: Harper & Row, Pubs., Inc.

Over the River and Through the Wood. Lydia M. Child. New York: Scholastic Book Services.

The Plymouth Thanksgiving. Leonard Weisgard. New York: Doubleday & Co., Inc.

BOOKS FOR TEACHERS

Nothing to Eat, But Food. Frank J. Tuppo. New York: E.P. Dutton Pub. Co., Inc.

BOOKS AND OTHER MEDIA

OTHER MEDIA
Filmstrips
Foods We Eat. Chicago: Society for Visual Education. Set of 6, 52 – 66 frames.

Holidays and Seasons. Mahwah, N.J.: Troll Associates. Set of 7.

Living on a Farm. Chicago: Coronet Instructional Films. Set of 6, 47 – 52 frames.

Films (16 mm)
Bread, 2nd ed. Chicago: Encyclopaedia Britannica Educational Corp. 11 min, color or b/w.

Food—From Farm to You. Indianapolis, Ind.: Farm Bureau. 15 min, optical sound, color.

Records
"Garden Song." *Silver Burdett Music 2,* Record 9.

"Let's Go to the Sea." *Silver Burdett Music 1,* Record 8.

"Mama Paquita." verse 1. *Silver Burdett Music 1,* Record 7.

CHAPTER FOUR
BOOKS FOR PUPILS
Animals Should Definitely Not Wear Clothing. Judith Barrett. New York: Atheneum Pubs.

Annie and the Old One. Misko Miles. Boston: Little, Brown & Co.

Barefoot Boy. Gloria D. Miklowitz. Chicago: Follett Pub. Co.

Belinda's New Shoes. Winifred Bromhall. New York: Alfred A. Knopf, Inc.

Cover-ups: Things to Put on Yourself. McPhee Gribble Pubs., ed. New York: Penguin Books.

Dirk's Wooden Shoes. Ilona Fennema and Georgette Apol. New York: Harcourt Brace Jovanovich, Inc.

The First Blue Jeans. Riki Dru. Contemporary Perspectives, Inc. (Distributed by Silver Burdett Co., Morristown, N.J.)

I Can Dress Myself. Dick Bruno. New York: Methuen, Inc.

Mrs. McGarrit's Peppermint Sweater. Adelaide Hall. New York: Lothrop, Lee & Shepard Books.

My Learn to Sew Book. Janet Barber. Racine, Wis.: Western Pub. Co., Inc.

Pelle's New Suit. Elsa Beskow. New York: Harper & Row, Pubs., Inc.

Snipp, Snapp, Snurr and the Red Shoes. Maj Lindman. Chicago: Albert Whitman & Co.

Try on a Shoe. June Belk Moncure. Child's World, P.O. Box 681, Elgin, Ill.

What Should I Wear? Pamela Rowland. Chicago: Childrens Press.

Who Puts the Blue in Jeans. Alice Edmond. New York: Random House, Inc.

BOOKS FOR TEACHERS
Clothes and Ornaments. Stephanie Thompson. New York: Macmillan Ltd. (Distributed by Silver Burdett Co., Morristown, N.J.)

The New World of Fabrics. Irmegnarde Eberle. New York: Dodd, Mead & Co.

Nothing to Wear But Clothes. Frank Jupo. New York: E.P. Dutton Pub. Co., Inc.

The Story of Clothes. 2nd ed. Agnes Allen. Salem, N.H.: Merrimack Book Services, Inc.

OTHER MEDIA
Filmstrips
Cotton Clothing from Field to You. Lakeland, Fla.: Imperial Films Co., Inc. Set of 6, 35 frames.

Families Need Clothing. Mahwah, N.J.: Troll Associates. 50 frames, record or cassette, color.

How We Get Our Clothing: The Story of Cotton; The Story of Wool. Chicago: Society for Visual Education, Inc. 33 – 35 frames.

Your Clothes. Chicago: Coronet Instructional Films. 49 frames, record, cassette or script, color.

Films
Cloth—Fiber to Fabric. Chicago: Encyclopaedia Britannica Corp. 15 min, optical sound, color or b/w.

Clothing—A Pair of Blue Jeans. New York: Learning Corp. of America. 15 min, optical sound, color.

Records
"Can You Guess What I Am?" *Silver Burdett Music, Early Childhood,* Record 2.

"I Had a Little Overcoat." *Silver Burdett Music 1,* Record 8.

"Mama Paquita," verse 2. *Silver Burdett Music 1,* Record 7.

"Sheep Shearing." *Silver Burdett Music 2,* Record 4.

"Threads." *Silver Burdett Music 1,* Record 7.

CHAPTER FIVE
BOOKS FOR PUPILS
Abraham Lincoln. Ingri D'Aulaire and Edgar Parin D'Aulaire. New York: Doubleday & Co., Inc.

The House of Four Seasons. Roger Duvoisin. New York: Lothrop, Lee & Shepard Books.

Kirt's New House. Calvin Cannon and Elaine Wickens. New York: Coward, McCann & Geoghegan, Inc.

The Little House. Virginia Burton. Boston: Houghton Mifflin Co.

Little House of Your Own. Beatrice DeRegniers and Irene Haas. New York: Harcourt Brace Jovanovich, Inc.

Little Igloo. Lorraine Beim and Jerrold Beim. New York: Harcourt Brace Jovanovich, Inc.

A Weed Is a Flower: The Life of George Washington Carver. Aliki. Englewood Cliffs, N.J.: Prentice-Hall, Inc.

BOOKS FOR TEACHERS
The City in History. Lewis Mumford. New York: Harcourt Brace Jovanovich, Inc.

Shelter and Society. Paul Oliver, ed. New York: Barrie & Jenkins.

OTHER MEDIA
Filmstrips
Shelter Is a Basic Need. Chicago: Encyclopaedia Britannica Educational Corp. 14 frames, captions, color.

Films (16 mm)
Shelter. Tucson, Ariz.: Gateway Productions, Inc. 10 min, optical sound.

Shelter—Almost Anyone Can Build a House. New York: Learning Corp. of America. 15 min, optical sound, color.

Records
"Bling Blang." *Silver Burdett Music 1,* Record 7.

"When You Live in a Lighthouse." *Silver Burdett Music 1,* Record 1.

CHAPTER SIX
BOOKS FOR PUPILS
Adam's ABC. Dale Fife. New York: Coward, McCann & Geoghegan, Inc.

The Bagel Baker of Mulliner Lane. Judith H. Blau and L. Dean. New York: McGraw-Hill, Inc.

Carol's Side of the Street. Lorraine Beim. New York: Harcourt Brace Jovanovich, Inc.

The City Book. Lucille Corcos. Racine, Wis.: Western Pub. Co., Inc.

City Poems. Lois Lenske. New York: Henry Z. Walch, Inc.

If I Built a Village. Kazue Mizumura. New York: Thomas Y. Crowell Co., Pubs.

It's Time Now. Alvin Tresselt. New York: Lothrop, Lee & Shepard Books.

The Little House. Virginia L. Burton. Boston: Houghton Mifflin Co.

Miss Terry at the Library, rev. ed. Jean Barr. Chicago: Albert Whitman & Co.

My Friend the Dentist. Jane W. Watson, et al. Racine, Wis.: Western Pub. Co., Inc.

Nice New Neighbors. Franz Brandenberg. New York: Greenwillow Books.

Nothing Ever Happens on my Block. Ellen Raskin. New York: Atheneum Pubs.

Open the Door and See all the People. Clyde R. Bulla. New York: Thomas Y. Crowell Co., Pubs.

The Tall Book of Nursery Tales. Feodor Rojankovsky. New York: Harper & Row, Pubs., Inc.

The Coming of the Pilgrims. Brooks E. Smith and Robert Meredith. Boston: Little, Brown & Co.

Feast of Thanksgiving. June Behrens. Chicago: Childrens Press.

First Poems of Childhood. Tasha Tudor. New York: Platt & Munk Pubs.

The First Thanksgiving. Lou Rogers. Chicago: Follett Pub. Co.

George Washington. Clara Judson. Chicago: Follett Pub. Co.

George Washington. Vivian L. Thompson. New York: G.P. Putnam's Sons.

Happy Birthday to You. Dr. Seuss. New York: Random House, Inc.

If You Grew Up with Abraham Lincoln. Ann McGovern. New York: Scholastic Book Services.

Jenny's Birthday Book. Esther H. Averill. New York: Harper & Row, Pubs., Inc.

Let's Find Out About Abraham Lincoln. Martha Shapp and Charles Shapp. New York: Franklin Watts, Inc.

Let's Find Out About Indians. Martha Shapp and Charles Shapp. New York: Franklin Watts, Inc.

Lincoln's Birthday. Clyde R. Bulla. New York: Thomas Y. Crowell Co., Pubs.

The Little Boy and the Birthdays. Helen E. Buckley. New York: Lothrop, Lee & Shepard Books.

Lyle and the Birthday Party. Waber Bernard. Boston: Houghton Mifflin Co.

A Man Named Washington. Gertrude Norman. New York: G.P. Putnam's Sons.

Martin Luther King, Jr. Margaret Jones. Chicago: Childrens Press.

Meet Abraham Lincoln. Barbara Cary. New York: Random House, Inc.

Meet Christopher Columbus. James DeKay. New York: Random House, Inc.

Meet George Washington. Joan Heilbroner. New York: Random House, Inc.

A New Flag for a New Country. June Behrens. Chicago: Childrens Press.

The Picture Life of Martin Luther King, Jr. Margaret B. Young. New York: Franklin Watts, Inc.

Thanksgiving Day. Robert M. Bartlett. New York: Thomas Y. Crowell Co., Pubs.

BOOKS FOR TEACHERS

The Book of Holidays, rev. ed. J. Walker McSpadden. New York: Thomas Y. Crowell Co., Pubs.

The First Book of Holidays. Bernice Burnett. New York: Franklin Watts, Inc.

Holidays Around the World. Joseph Gaer. Boston: Little, Brown & Co.

Pumpkins, Pinwheels and Peppermint Packages: Teacher's Edition. Imogene Forte and others. Nashville, Tenn.: Incentive Pubs., Inc.

The Story of the Declaration of Independence. Norman Richards. Chicago: Childrens Press.

The Story of the 13 Colonies. Clifford Alderman. New York: Random House, Inc.

OTHER MEDIA
Filmstrips

Americans Who Shaped History. Mahwah, N.J.: Troll Associates. Set of 6, 41 – 43 Frames.

Great American Presidents. Chicago: Society for Visual Education. Set of 5, 28 – 35 frames.

Holidays American Style. Baldwin, N.Y.: Activity Records. Set of 6.

Holidays and Special Days. New York: Learning Corp. of America. Set of 6, 48 – 68 frames, cassette, color.

Let's Celebrate Holidays. Mahwah, N.J.: Troll Associates. Set of 6, 39 frames.

Lincoln and Washington: Why We Celebrate Their Birthdays. Chicago: Society for Visual Education. Set of 2, 42 – 45 frames.

People and Events in American History. Pomfret, Conn.: Communicators. Set of 6, 29 – 38 frames.

Thanksgiving for King. Chicago: Society for Visual Education. 37 frames, record or cassette, color.

Films (16 mm)

America's Heroes: Abraham Lincoln. Chicago: Coronet Instructional Films. 11 min, optical sound.

America's Heroes: George Washington. Chicago: Coronet Instructional Films. 11 min, optical sound.

The Boyhood of Abraham Lincoln. Chicago: Coronet Instructional Films. 11 min, optical sound.

The Boyhood of George Washington. Chicago: Coronet Instructional Films. 8 min, optical sound.

Records

"The Band in the Square." *Silver Burdett Music 2,* Record 3.

PROFESSIONAL BOOKS FOR TEACHERS

The Blue Book of Occupational Education. Max M. Russell, ed. New York: CCM Information Corporation.

Crucial Issues in the Teaching of Social Studies: A Book of Readings. Byron G. Massialas and Andreas M. Kazamais, eds. Englewood Cliffs, N.J.: Prentice-Hall, Inc.

Discovering the Structure of Social Studies. James G. Womack. Encino, Calif.: Bruce & Glencoe, Inc.

Economics and Its Significance. Richard S. Martin and Reuben G. Miller. Columbus, Ohio: Charles E. Merrill Pub. Co.

The Geography of Population: A Teacher's Guide. Paul Griffin, ed. The 1970 Yearbook of The National Council for Geographic Education. Belmont, Calif.: Fearon Pubs., Inc.

Handicapped People in Society: Ideas and Activities for Teachers. Ruth-Ellen K. Ross, and others. Morristown, N.J.: Silver Burdett Company.

Skill Development in Social Studies. (Thirty-third Yearbook of the National Council for the Social Studies). Helen McCracken Carpenter, ed. Washington, D.C.: National Council for the Social Studies.

The Slow Learner in the Classroom. Newell C. Kephart. Columbus, Ohio: Charles E. Merrill Pub. Co.

The Social Studies and the Social Sciences. Gordon B. Turner, et al. New York: Harcourt Brace Jovanovich, Inc.

The Social Studies: Eightieth Yearbook of the National Society for the Study of Education, Part II. Howard D. Mehlinger and O. L. Davis, Jr., eds. Chicago: University of Chicago Press.

Social Studies Through Problem Solving. Maxine Dunfee and Helen Sagl. New York: Holt, Rinehart & Winston, Inc.

Sociology: The Study of Man in Society. Caroline B. Rose. Columbus, Ohio: Charles E. Merrill Pub. Co.

The Study and Teaching of Social Science Series. Raymond H. Muessig, ed. New York: Charles E. Merrill Pub. Co.

Teaching Ethnic Studies. James A. Banks, ed. Belmont, Calif.: Fearon Pubs., Inc.

Teaching Social Studies in the Elementary School. Theodore Kaltsounis. Englewood Cliffs, N.J.: Prentice-Hall, Inc.

The World and Its People
NEIGHBORHOODS AND COMMUNITIES

The World and Its People

AUTHORS

Val E. Arnsdorf, Professor,
  College of Education, University of Delaware,
  Newark, Delaware
Carolyn S. Brown, Principal,
  Robertson Academy School, Nashville, Tennessee
Kenneth S. Cooper, Professor of History, Emeritus,
  George Peabody College for Teachers, Vanderbilt
  University, Nashville, Tennessee
Alvis T. Harthern, Professor of Education,
  University of Montevallo, Montevallo, Alabama
Timothy M. Helmus, Middle School Teacher,
  Harrison Park Middle School, Grand Rapids,
  Michigan
Bobbie P. Hyder, Elementary Education Coordinator,
  Madison County School System, Huntsville, Alabama
Theodore Kaltsounis, Professor and Chairman of
  Curriculum and Instruction,
  College of Education, University of Washington,
  Seattle, Washington
Richard H. Loftin, Director of Curriculum and Staff
  Development,
  Aldine Independent School District, Houston, Texas
Norman J. G. Pounds, Former University Professor
  of Geography,
  Indiana University, Bloomington, Indiana
Edgar A. Toppin, Professor of History and Dean of
  the Graduate School,
  Virginia State University, Petersburg, Virginia

PROGRAM CONTRIBUTORS

Paula Allaert, Third Grade Teacher,
  St. Therese School, Portland, Oregon
Carol Armour, Third Grade Teacher,
  Marie V. Duffy Elementary School, Wharton, New Jersey
Sandra Breman, Fifth Grade Teacher,
  Whitney Young Magnet School, Fort Wayne, Indiana
Vivian Brown, Fifth Grade Teacher,
  Silver Spur Elementary School, Rancho Palos Verdes,
  California
Kim Eyler, Former Elementary School Teacher,
  Wyckoff, New Jersey
Sharon Gaydon, Sixth Grade Teacher,
  Thompson Middle School, Alabaster, Alabama
Janet Glenn, Second Grade Teacher,
  Greene School, Greensboro, North Carolina
Viola Gonzalez, Fifth-Sixth Grade Teacher,
  Ryan Elementary School, Laredo, Texas
Ellen Gremillion, Third Grade Teacher,
  Parkview Elementary School, Baton Rouge, Louisiana
Lucy Hatch, Fifth-Sixth Grade Teacher,
  Taylor Elementary School, Abilene, Texas
Judy Hobson, Fourth Grade Teacher,
  Elmdale Elementary School, Springdale, Arkansas
Peggy Hogg, Fourth Grade Teacher,
  Dartmouth Elementary School, Richardson, Texas
Geoffrey Kashdan, Special Education Teacher,
  Hanover Avenue School, Morris Plains, New Jersey
Gloria Lemos, First Grade Teacher,
  Emerson Elementary School, Pasco, Washington
William Lentino, Fifth Grade Teacher,
  Lloyd Harbor Elementary School, Huntington, New York
Carolyn Lombardo, Third Grade Teacher,
  Ferrara Elementary School, East Haven, Connecticut
Mary Lou Martin, Social Studies Resource Teacher, K–6,
  San Diego Unified School District, San Diego, California
Patricia McWey, Second Grade Teacher,
  Martin Luther King School, Providence, Rhode Island
Sandra Murphy Mead, Second Grade Teacher,
  L. W. West School, Endicott, New York
Ray Ringley, Fifth Grade Teacher,
  Powell Valley Primary School, Big Stone Gap, Virginia
Elaine Sisselman, Fourth Grade Teacher,
  Biscayne Gardens Elementary School, Miami, Florida
Katharyn Smith, First Grade Teacher,
  The Meadows School, College Park, Georgia
Jan Talbot, Sixth Grade Teacher,
  Pope Avenue Elementary School, Sacto, California
Patricia Terai, First Grade Teacher,
  Woodin Elementary School, Bothell, Washington
William Tucker, Sixth Grade Teacher,
  Alanton Elementary School, Virginia Beach, Virginia
Sister Catherine Zajac, S.S.J., Fourth-Sixth Grade Teacher,
  St. Agnes School, Dalton, Massachusetts

NEIGHBORHOODS AND COMMUNITIES

BOBBIE P. HYDER   Elementary Education Coordinator
Madison County School System, Huntsville, Alabama

CAROLYN S. BROWN   Principal
Robertson Academy School, Nashville, Tennessee

SILVER BURDETT COMPANY   Morristown, N.J.
Glenview, Ill. • San Carlos, Calif. • Dallas • Atlanta

CONTENTS

MAPS

END-OF-CHAPTER SKILLS DEVELOPMENT

A LETTER TO YOU FROM THE AUTHORS

Dear Student,

Do you know what the earth is made of? Can you name the different kinds of land? Do you know how many continents there are? The answers to these questions can be found in this book, Neighborhoods and Communities.

This year you will be using Neighborhoods and Communities, a social studies textbook. This makes us very happy. We worked hard to make this a good book for you.

In this book you will discover many things about family life in communities. You will also learn about the many kinds of work people do, special days and how families celebrate them, why people need rules and laws, and many other exciting things.

We hope you and your classmates will enjoy learning about our home, the earth, and about the people who live here.

Sincerely,

Bobbie P. Hyder

Carolyn Saunders Brown

CHAPTER 1

Where We Live

If I could choose a country
That would be best for me,
I'd first choose one with lots of space
To grow and learn and be.

I'd want one with big cities
And towns and farmland, too,
Great plains and soaring mountains
With rivers running through.

There would be room for forests
And deserts painted bright.
What would I call my country?
"America" sounds just right!

Read the poem to the class.

Yosemite National Park in California

1

Point out that the earth is made up of large bodies of land and large
bodies of water. Some land is covered with trees and other kinds of
vegetation.

We live on the <u>earth</u>.
The earth is our home.
These pictures show part of our home.
The earth is the home of all people.
The earth is made of land and water.

water

The parts of the earth that are not covered by land are covered with water. About ⅔ of the earth's surface is covered with water.

3

Wildflowers add to the beauty of the earth. Point out the narrow road. Ask: Why do you think the road is there?

The earth is very large. Many different kinds of plants and animals live on the earth.

These deer are one of the many kinds of animals that live on the earth. Ask: Where do you think these deer live? What are these deer doing?

4

People live all over the earth. People are alike in some ways and different in other ways.

There are many different kinds of people, too.

Discuss some differences such as height, weight and age. Also some likenesses.

People live on different kinds of land.
Some people live on flat land called <u>plains</u>.
There are few trees on the plains.
This is good land for farming.

Stress that all land is not alike. This is flat land. It is good for farming.
These farmers are harvesting oats. Oats are an important grain. Ask:
What are some other grains? What are some foods that are made from
grains?

The machine in the foreground cuts the stalks and separates the grains of oats.

6

Some people live on hilly land.
<u>Hills</u> are higher than plains.
Sometimes trees grow on the sides of hills.

Some land is hilly. A hill is higher than the land around it.

Other people live on <u>mountains</u>. Mountains are very big hills. They rise high above the land around them. Snow covers the tops of the highest mountains.

Mountains are high. Some are covered with trees. Some are steep and rocky. Ask: Do you live near a mountain?

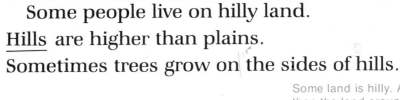

snow-covered mountains

7

sand castle

Many people live near <u>oceans</u>.
Oceans are large bodies of water.
People fish in the ocean.
They like to swim in the ocean, too.

The strip of land beside the ocean is called a beach.

Much of the earth's surface is water. The largest bodies of water are called oceans. Water in the ocean is salty. Many kinds of plants and animals live in the oceans. Ask: Why do some people like to live near oceans?

Some people live near <u>rivers</u>.
A river is a long body of water that
flows through the land.
This big river is the Mississippi River.

Explain that rivers are smaller than oceans. Long ago riverboats were an important means of transportation. Today people take sightseeing trips on the riverboat *Delta Queen*.

Some people live near <u>lakes</u>.
A lake is a body of water with land all around it.
People have fun sailing and rowing boats on lakes.

Have pupils start a discussion about where they live. Ask: What does the earth look like where you live? Is there water nearby? How is the earth where we live the same as the pictures on pages 6–9?

Other people live on land that has water all around it. This land is called an <u>island</u>. Point to the island in the picture.

Point out that some islands are too small for people to live on. Some are very large. Hawaii is a large island.

Some people live on a <u>peninsula</u>. A peninsula is land that has water nearly all the way around it. It is part of a larger body of land.
Trace the peninsula with your finger.

Tell pupils to find the peninsula and trace with their finger the shape of the peninsula. Have them point to the body of land to which the peninsula is attached.

This picture shows the different parts of the earth.
Point to each one in the drawing.

plain	lake
hills	river
mountains	island
ocean	peninsula

boat docks

baseball diamond

Notice how different the earth looks from an airplane.
Ask: Can you find an island in the picture?

The picture on this page was taken
from an airplane. It shows what the earth
looks like from the air.

Look at the <u>map</u> on the next page.
A map is a drawing of the earth
or part of the earth.
This map shows the same place
that the picture shows.

Have pupils put a sheet of paper over the map on p. 13.
Ask them to name the features they recognize in the
picture above (a baseball field, streets, houses, a ten-
nis court, a lake). List the features on the chalkboard.
Now have pupils uncover the map and cover the picture on p. 12. Without referring to the list, have pupils
tell as much as they can about the area from the map
and from their recollection of the photograph.

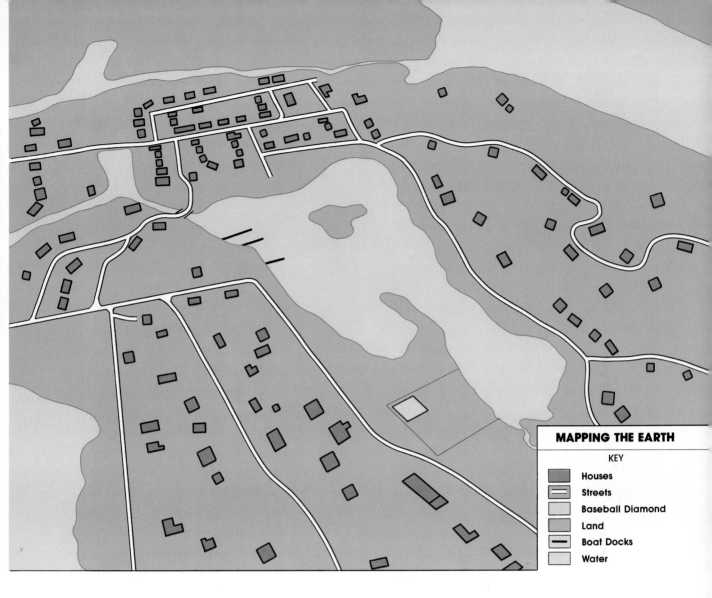

MAPPING THE EARTH

KEY

- Houses
- Streets
- Baseball Diamond
- Land
- Boat Docks
- Water

How are the picture and the map
like each other?
How are they different from each other?
The map has <u>symbols</u>.
Symbols stand for real things.
They stand for real places.
The <u>key</u> tells what the symbols stand for.
Name the symbols on the map.

This is a picture of the earth.
It was taken from far out in space.
It shows that the earth is round.
The earth is shaped like a ball.

This is how the earth looks from space.
Ask: What shape is the earth?

This is a picture of a <u>globe</u>.

A globe is a <u>model</u> of the earth.

It shows the oceans and the land.

The oceans are blue. What color is the land?

People use the globe to find different places on the earth.

The <u>North Pole</u> is a very special place.
It is the most northern place on the earth.
<u>North</u> is the <u>direction</u> toward the North Pole.
Put your finger on the North Pole.

THE NORTH POLE

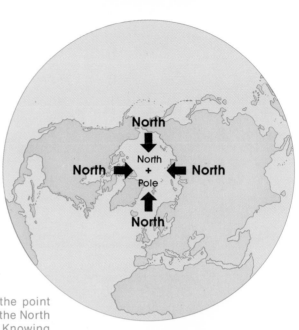

Point out that the earth has a North Pole. It is the point farthest north on the earth. The boy is pointing to the North Pole on the globe. Stress that north is a direction. Knowing where north is helps one to find other directions.

16

The South Pole is another very special place. It is the most southern place on the earth. South is the direction toward the South Pole. Put your finger on the South Pole. The South Pole is opposite the North Pole.

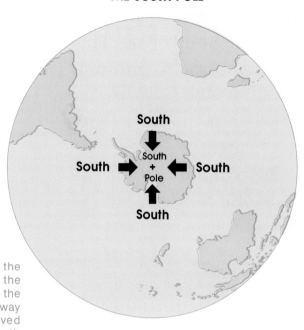

South
South
South + Pole
South
South

South is opposite north. Ask: Where is the South Pole on the globe? Have pupils take turns finding the South Pole on the globe. Have a pupil place a finger on the North Pole. Tell the pupil to move his or her hand slowly down the globe, away from the North Pole. Ask: In what direction have you moved your finger? Stress that when moving away from the North Pole, the only direction is south.

Very few people have ever been to the North Pole
or the South Pole. The first people were <u>explorers</u>.
They came to find new places.

Explorers are people who go in search of new lands.

The pictures on this page
show the first explorers to
reach the North Pole and the
South Pole.

The South Pole was first reached in 1911.
The North Pole was first reached in 1909.

Matthew Henson and Robert E. Peary were members of the
first expedition to reach the North Pole in 1909.

18

Today people still explore the North and South Poles. Snowmobiles and dog teams travel over the frozen ground.

The weather at the Poles is very cold. Even in summer the ground remains frozen.

This ship is called an Icebreaker.
It breaks through the ice and opens a path
for other ships.

ice

FOUR DIRECTIONS

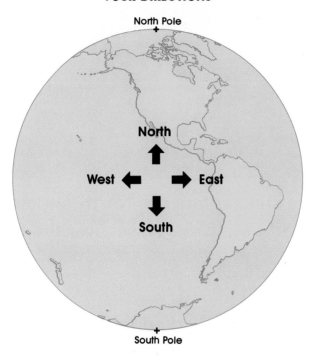

North and south are directions.
Two other directions are <u>east</u> and <u>west</u>.
Find east and west on the globe.

Use a flat compass to find the cardinal directions in your classroom. First explain what a compass is. Then let pupils hold the compass and discover what happens to the needle if they turn to the right or left, if they make a complete turn, or if they walk to the corner of the room. Stress that no matter which way the compass case is turned, the needle always points in the same direction. Ask: In what direction does the needle point?

NORTH

The sun seems to rise in the east and to set in the west. When you face north, east is to your right and west is to your left. East and west are opposite each other.

WEST

EAST

SOUTH

THE EARTH'S CONTINENTS

This map shows the whole earth.
The land on the earth is divided into <u>continents</u>.
A continent is a large body of land.

There are seven continents.
Find each continent on the map.
   This map also shows the oceans of the earth.

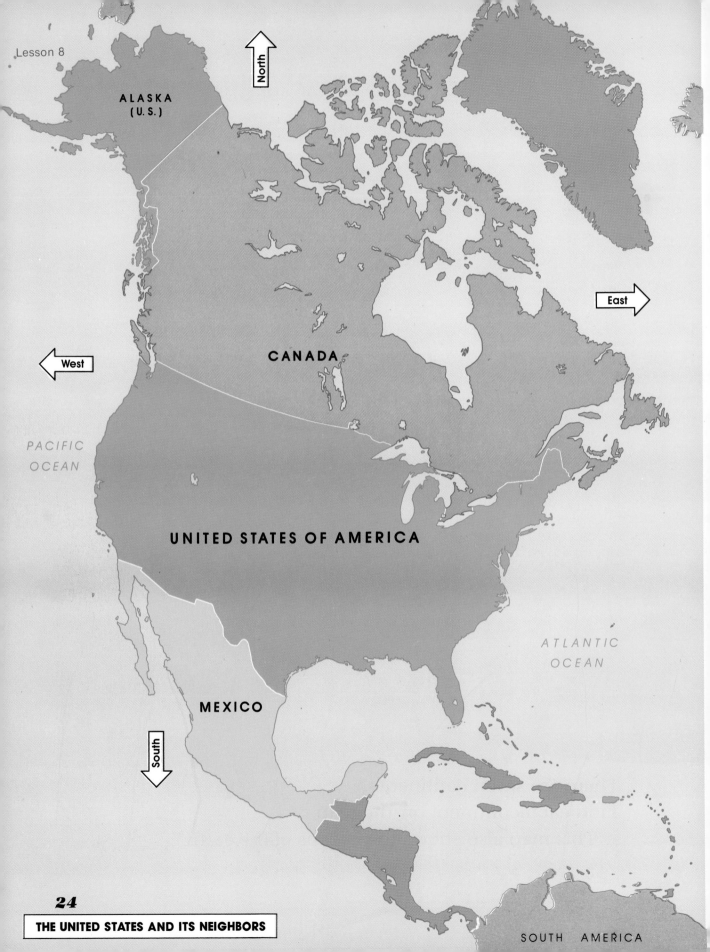

North

East

West

ALASKA
(U.S.)

CANADA

PACIFIC
OCEAN

UNITED STATES OF AMERICA

ATLANTIC
OCEAN

MEXICO

South

THE UNITED STATES AND ITS NEIGHBORS

SOUTH AMERICA

On this map you see the continent of North America. The United States is one country in North America. We live in the United States. Find it on the map.

Mexico is south of the United States. It is also a country in North America.

Another country in North America is Canada. Find Canada on the map. It is our neighbor to the north.

Each country has a flag. People have a special feeling for their flag. The flag is a symbol. It stands for their country.

These boys are putting up the flag in their schoolyard. Tell pupils that all American schools fly the flag.

Have pupils describe the United States flag. Now would be a good time to explain the significance of the number of stars and stripes.

Help pupils understand that saluting the American flag is one way that people show honor and respect for their country.

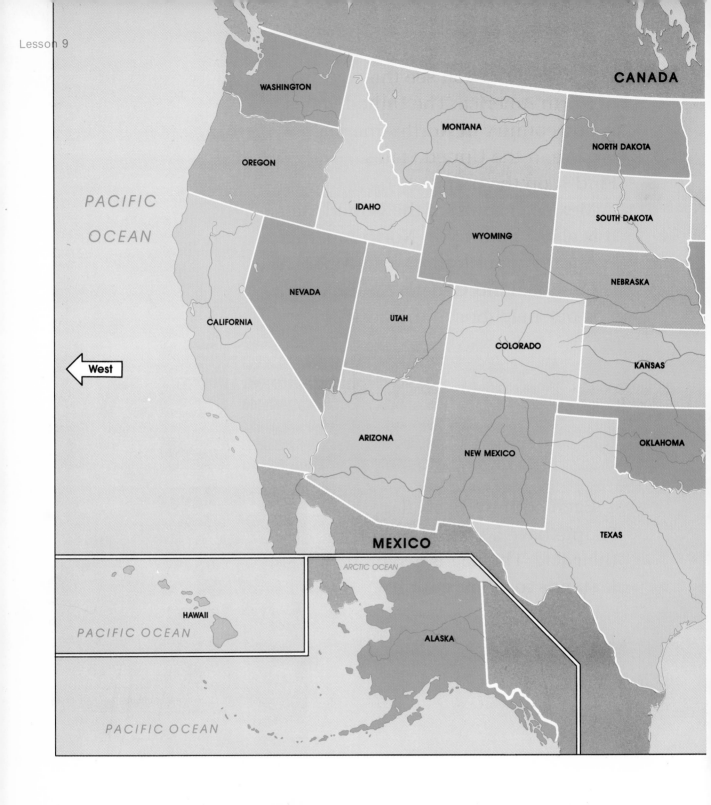

This is a map of our country. The United States is divided into 50 <u>states</u>. Each state has a name. Find your state on the map.

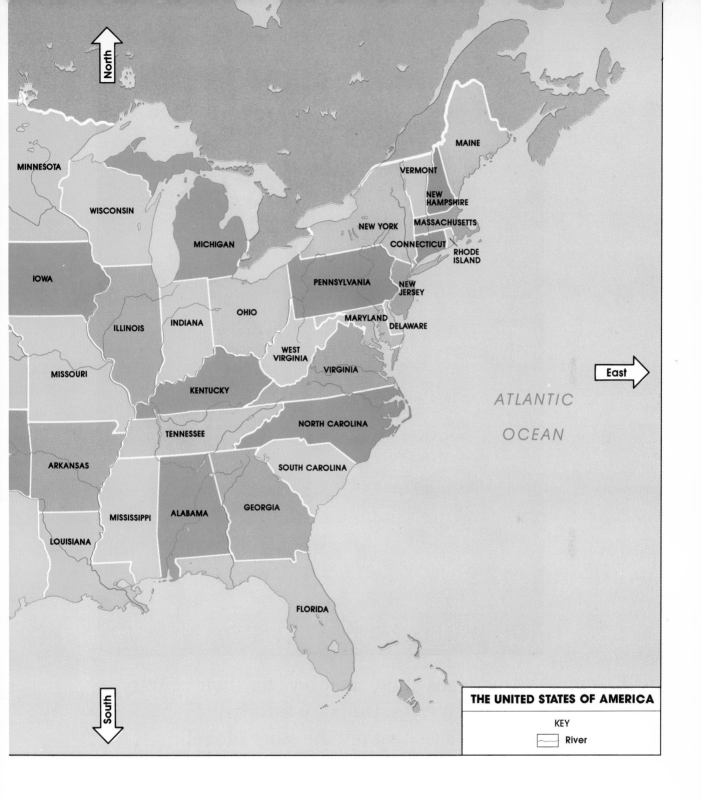

The United States has another name. It is America.
The people in our country are called Americans.
They are proud of their country.

Americans show their love for their country in different ways. One way is to visit special places that tell the story of their country. Another way is to sing songs about their country. You might like to learn a song. It is about the land that is our home. It is about the United States of America.

The Washington Monument is named for George Washington, our first President. This monument is in Washington, D.C.

THIS LAND IS YOUR LAND

WORDS AND MUSIC BY WOODY GUTHRIE   COUNTERMELODY BY RUTH TUTELMAN

REFRAIN

This land is your land,_____ this land is my land,_____

From Ca - li - for - nia_____ to the New York is - land;_____

From the red - wood for - est_____ to the Gulf Stream wa - ters;_____

This land was made for you and me._____

VERSE

1. As I was walk - ing_____ that rib - bon of high - way,_____

I saw a - bove me_____ that end - less sky - way._____

I saw be - low me_____ that gold - en val - ley,_____

This land was made for you and me._____

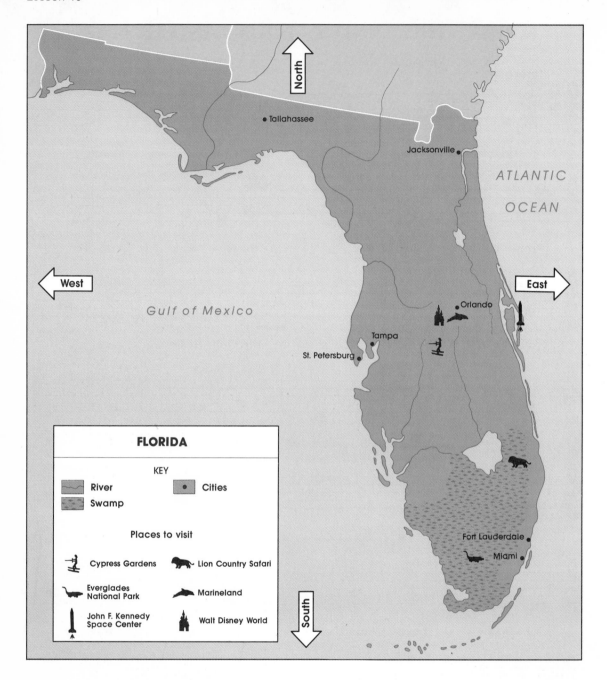

This is a map of Florida.
Florida is one of our 50 states.
Many people visit Florida. The map key
shows you some of the places people go to see.

30

Disney World

Everglades National Park

Cypress Gardens

Lion Country Safari

Marineland

whale

Kennedy Space Center

Have you ever visited any places in Florida?

Have pupils find the pictures that match the places shown in the map key.

31

tree

sand

The mockingbird is the State bird of Florida.
The State flower is the orange blossom.

Each state has a nickname. Each state also
has a special bird and a special flower.

The nickname for Florida is the Sunshine State.
It is called that because it has so many sunny days.
The State bird and the State flower of Florida
are shown on this page.

Find the nickname, bird, and flower for your state.

Divide the class into small groups. Have each group choose a state and find out the
nickname, flower, and bird for that state. One group should find out this information
about the pupils' own state. Have each group make a poster showing the state's name,
nickname, and drawings of the state bird and the state flower.

Ask: How are these two communities the same? How are they different? Do either one of the communities look like our community in any way?

This is an aerial view of Miami. It is a large community.

Each state has cities and towns. People call their city or town their community.

These pictures show communities in Florida. Some communities are large. Some are small.

All communities have names. Find the names of some communities in Florida on the map on page 30.

This is Naples. It is a small community.

33

KEY FACTS

1. The earth is made of land and water. There is land and water of many different shapes and sizes.

2. A map is a drawing of any part of the earth.

3. A globe is a model of the earth.

4. North, south, east, and west are directions. Directions help people find places.

5. We live on the continent of North America.

6. Our country is the United States of America. It is divided into 50 states.

VOCABULARY QUIZ

Number your paper from 1 to 6.
Write the word that matches each picture.

island

peninsula

lake

plain

mountain

river

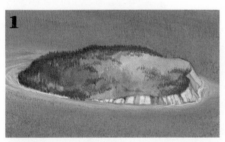

REVIEW QUESTIONS

1. What are some things that live on earth?

2. What is an island?

3. What is a peninsula?

4. What does a key on a map tell us?

5. What does a globe show us about the earth?

6. If you know which way north is, how can you find east? How can you find west?

7. What is a continent?

8. Where is the country of Mexico? Where is Canada?

9. Why do people have special feelings for their flag?

ACTIVITIES

1. Make a map of your classroom. Draw symbols to show the different things in the room. Be sure you make a key for the map. The map on page 13 can help you make your map.

2. Pretend you are up in space looking at the earth. Draw a picture of the earth.

3. Make a list of some of the things you like about the United States.

Answers to review questions:
1. People, animals, plants
2. Land surrounded by water
3. Land almost completely surrounded by water
4. What symbols on a map stand for
5. Where places are on earth; the earth is round.
6. East is to your right; west is to your left.
7. One of seven large bodies of land
8. Mexico is south of the United States.
   Canada is north of the United States.
9. The flag is a symbol of their country.

Using Map Directions

Directions help us find places on maps and globes.

This is a map of a park. Use the map to answer the questions.

Write your answers on a sheet of paper.

1. Make believe you are walking in the Park Entrance. Is the Roller Coaster south or east of the entrance?   east

2. Is the Flower Garden north or south of the Haunted House?   south

3. Is Silver Lake east or west of the Zoo?   west

4. Are the Magic Mountains north or south of the Pony Rides?   north

5. Is the Picnic Area east or west of the Merry-Go-Round?   west

6. Is the Information Booth north or south of the Park Entrance?   north

7. Is the Park Gift Shop west or east of the Pony Rides?   west

May I visit your community?
Do you think it looks like mine?
Do you have a school quite close to home?
Does your school bell ring at nine?

May I visit your community?
Do you have a park nearby?
Do you ever have a local fair
With rides and kites to fly?

May I visit your community?
Could I get there on my bike?
Why not come to visit me?
I'll show you things you'll like!

Call on pupils to read the poem. Ask: Have you ever been to
a fair or a festival?

Ninth Avenue food festival in New York City

Communities are made up of people and buildings. Point out that communities differ in size and in the number of people living in them. Have pupils find some differences and similarities between the communities on these pages. Point out things such as land, water, trees, grass, a street light, and a mailbox. Help pupils understand that each community is important to the American way of life.

A community is a place where people live. There are many kinds of communities. Some are large. Some are small.

40

fishing community

lobster traps

This is a farm. A group of farms make up a farming community. Ask: How can you tell it is early morning? From which direction does the sun seem to rise?

sun

barn

41

The people in these pictures
live near each other. They are <u>neighbors</u>.
They live in the same <u>neighborhood</u>.
A group of neighborhoods
make up a community.

Neighbors sometimes help each other.
They work together to clean up
their neighborhood.

Point out that neighbors are often friends, and that they work together to make their neighborhood a nice place to live. Raise the question about what pupils can do to help keep their neighborhood a nice place to live. Raise the question about what pupils can do to help keep their neighborhood clean.

42

Ask: What are these neighbors doing? Do you think they are having fun? How can you tell? What season of the year is it?

Neighbors can have fun together.
What do you do
in your neighborhood?

Vacant lots like this can be turned into gardens or play areas.

43

This house is for one family.

A community has many kinds
of places for people to live.
Some people live in houses
made for one family.

Some people live in houses
made for many families.
They are called apartment
buildings.
Families share these buildings
with other families.
Apartment buildings come
in many shapes and sizes.
Find the apartment buildings
on these pages.

This house is for many families.

44

These are apartment buildings, too. Ask: How are they different from the apartment building on page 44?

If a community is near a lake or river, some people may live on houseboats. In some communities people live in house trailers.

What kinds of houses are in your community?

Houseboats are homes on water. Some families live on houseboats year round. Others use them for vacationing.

House trailers can be moved from place to place.

Tell pupils that most communities, large and small, have schools. Ask: What kind of community is this school in? What are the children doing? Do all schools have a lot of space and trees?

Communities have schools.
Schools are buildings set aside for learning.
Some schools are big. Some are small.
What does your school look like?
Long ago people did not have schools.
Children were taught to read and write at home.
Today the United States has many schools.
Children learn many things.
They learn about people in other parts of the world.
They learn skills that will help them
become good <u>citizens</u>.

Ask: Where are these children playing? Explain that in some large communities, the playground is on the roof of the school.

In some communities children walk to school. They also ride bicycles. In other communities children ride on a school bus.

Children who do not live near their school can ride the school bus.

What do you think the children in these pictures are learning?

48

These children are learning about science. Ask: What are some other things you learn in school?

The teacher is using maps to teach pupils about their community and state.

Many kinds of stores can be found
in communities. Some stores sell clothes.
Some stores sell food.
Clothes and food are <u>goods</u>.
What goods do you see in these pictures?

Ask: Are there stores in your community? What kinds of goods can
be bought in your community?

These buildings are also part of a community.
Can you name them?

Ask: What kinds of work do firefighters do?

Point out that many communities have a library. People can borrow books, pictures, and films. This would be a good time to take pupils on a tour of the school library.

Explain that people go to a hospital when they are sick. Ask: Who is the person in the picture? What do nurses do? This nurse is blind. A guide dog helps the nurse get around.

mail slot

directing traffic

The people in these pictures work for the community.
They provide <u>services</u> to people living in the community.

collecting garbage

Can you name the service each worker provides?

librarian

firefighters

Communities have places where people can have fun.
This is a park. Some people like to walk in a park.
What do you like to do in a park?

People of all ages can enjoy a park.
Point out the cherry trees in bloom.

space museum

Some people like to visit
a <u>museum</u>. At a museum you
can learn about many things.
You can learn about people
who lived a long time ago.
You can also learn about
the future.

Buses bring visitors to the museum.

56

This is a special kind of zoo where people can pet some of the animals. Stress that in most zoos petting is not allowed. Ask: What animals have you seen at the zoo?

Going to a zoo can also be fun.

Name some places where you can learn and have fun at the same time.

Hudson River

Communities come in many sizes. A large community is called a <u>city</u>.

This is New York City. It is the largest city in the United States.

A city has many places where people live and work. Some people work in small stores. Some work in tall office buildings.

Cities have many places for people to live, work, and shop. Ships bring goods from all over the world to New York Harbor.

An office worker may use a <u>typewriter</u>. A typewriter is a machine that makes letters on paper.

58

Empire State Building

Some people work in a <u>factory</u>. They make goods. These factory workers are making toys.

This man works in an office building in a city.

assembly line

59

This community is located
just outside a city. It is a <u>suburb</u>.
Most suburbs are smaller than cities.
They have fewer people than cities.

Suburbs do not have as many places for people to work as cities.

People who live in a suburb often work in the city.
They must have <u>transportation</u> to get there.
Some people use cars.
Some people use trains and buses to get around.

farmland

Some communities have few people but a lot of land.
They are <u>rural communities</u>.

Most people in rural communities work on farms.
They grow crops and raise animals.
Most of our food comes from rural communities.

62

Farm families go to communities like this to get the goods and services they need.

Some rural communities are near cities. Others are near <u>towns</u>. Many of these towns are small communities with few homes and stores. Some towns have grown up around farming communities.

63

There are communities in many different places.
Some communities are near the ocean.
Some are near mountains.
Others are near lakes and rivers.
A state is made up of many communities.
Look at the map. It shows the state of Indiana.
Symbols on the map show some of the towns and cities.
Which symbol stands for towns?
Which symbol stands for cities?
A map can help you learn about the towns
and cities in your state.

Have pupils look at the map key on the next page and find the symbol used
to show a city. Ask pupils to point to the city on the map that is farthest
north, south, east, and west. Ask: How many cities are on the map? How
many towns are on the map?

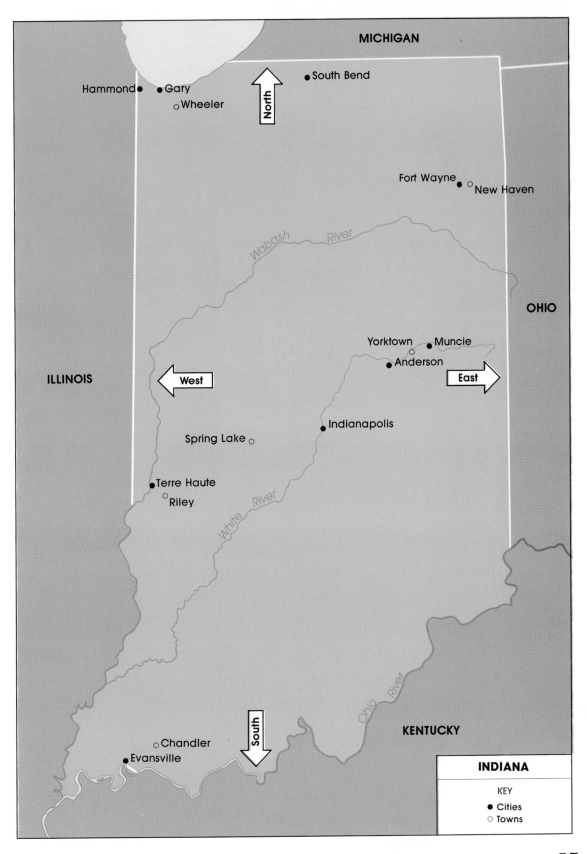

MICHIGAN

Hammond● ●Gary
○Wheeler
●South Bend

North

Fort Wayne● ○New Haven

OHIO

Yorktown ●Muncie
○
●Anderson

West

East

●Indianapolis

ILLINOIS

Spring Lake ○

●Terre Haute
○Riley

Wabash River

White River

South

Ohio River

KENTUCKY

○Chandler
●Evansville

INDIANA

KEY
● Cities
○ Towns

Communities are made up of people.
People come from all over the world
to live in the United States.
They live in many different communities.
They have different ways of doing things.
People in communities work and play together.

Tell pupils that there are many reasons why families move from one community to another. The major reason is that people live where they can find jobs. Point out that some people move to another community when they retire. Ask: Do any of you have grandparents who have moved to a senior citizens' community? Find out if any pupils in the class are new to the community. Ask them what kind of community they moved from.

Tell pupils that each year families from other countries come to the United States to live.

67

KEY FACTS

1. A community is a place where people live.
2. People who live near one another are neighbors.
3. Some communities are large and some are small.
4. Communities have many kinds of houses and buildings.
5. Communities have places where people can work, have fun, and learn.
6. People come from all over the world to live in the United States.

VOCABULARY QUIZ

Number your paper from 1 to 6.
Choose the right word for each sentence.

town   goods   service
city   houseboat   transportation

1. Food and clothes are ____goods____ .
2. A ____city____ is a large community.
3. A ____town____ is a community with few homes and stores.
4. People need __transportation__ to get around.
5. Collecting trash is a ____service____ .
6. A ____houseboat____ is a home on water.

REVIEW QUESTIONS

1. What are people who live in the same neighborhood called? neighbors

2. What kind of shelter can many families live in? apartment building

3. What kind of shelter can be moved from one place to another? trailer

4. Why do children go to school? to learn

5. What are goods? things that are made or grown

6. What are services? things that people do for others

7. Name some places in a community where families go to have fun. Answers will vary.

8. What are communities outside a city called? suburbs

9. What are communities with few homes and stores called? towns

ACTIVITIES

1. Pretend you and your family are moving to a new community.
Find pictures of the kinds of buildings you would like in your new community.

2. Draw a picture of a service worker your family depends on.

READING A MAP

Many families live in apartment buildings.
They share the buildings with other families.
The map shows one family's home in a
large apartment building. It shows
the size and shape of each room. Study the
map and answer the following questions.
Write your answers on a separate sheet
of paper.

1. How many rooms are in this home?
2. On which side of the map is the bathroom?
3. How many bedrooms are there?
4. Imagine you are in the dining room, in
which direction would you walk to get to
the living room?

Draw a map of your own home and label the rooms.

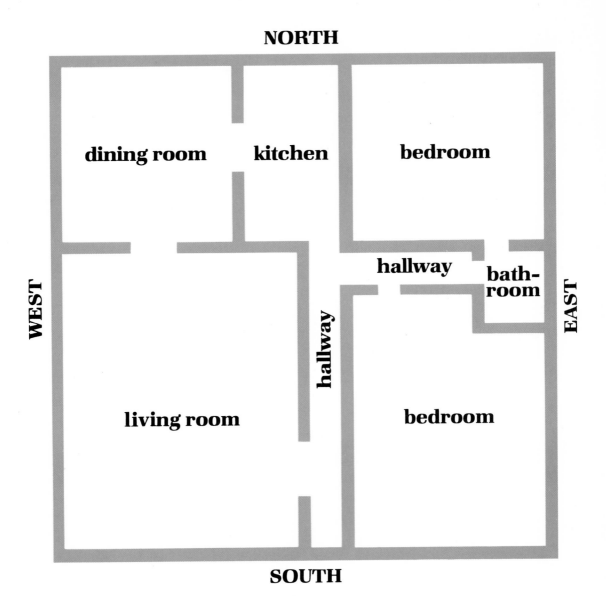

My Uncle Charlie cleans the streets,
My Auntie Lou sells bread and meats,
My sister May works in a bank,
Across the aisle from my brother Hank
My mom works in a tailor shop,
My dad is now a traffic cop.
I also have some work to do,
I go to school from nine till two.
We're all as proud as proud can be
To work in our community.

Call on pupils to read the poem.

People have <u>needs</u>.
Needs are things people cannot
do without.

People have <u>wants</u>.
Wants are things people like to have
but can do without.

Look at the pictures.

Which are needs? Which are wants?

74

Explain that there are some things people need, and some things people want. Call on pupils to name some things they want. Write the names of the items on the chalkboard. Discuss each item. Ask: Do you need this to live? Do all people need this? Is it a want or a need?

All people have the same basic needs.
The three basic needs are food, clothes
and shelter. People must have
these three things to live.

Tell pupils that food, clothes, and shelter are usually determined by the climate, the location, and the customs of the people living there.

People need more than food, clothes, and shelter.
They need love and affection.
They need friends.
They need to have fun.

78

Can you think of some other things people need?

Point out that people have other needs in addition to basic needs, but all people do not need the same things. Direct pupils' attention to the two children in the picture. Ask: Can you find something that one child needs and the other does not? (Glasses) Ask pupils to name some other things some people need and others do not.

People work to earn money. The money they earn is called <u>income</u>. Income is used to buy needs and wants.

Most people need jobs to earn money.

These workers are picking pineapples in Hawaii.

office worker

automobile factory

pizza maker

carpenter

What jobs are these people doing to earn money?

People get money for the work they do.

Communities must provide places for people to work.

Point out that all these workers will use their income to buy the things they need and want.

The things workers make or grow are called <u>goods</u>.

Look at the pictures on these pages.

These workers are making crayons.

They use machines to help them do their job.

Workers who grow goods usually work on farms. Workers who made goods usually work in factories or plants.

This worker must know how much powder to add to the wax.

This worker is adding red powder to melted wax.

The machine mixes the powder and wax.

82

This molding machine has 2,426 separate crayon-shaped molds.

The red wax is then taken from this machine.
It is put into another machine.
The wax is poured into holes.
It cools and hardens there.
The extra wax is scraped away.

A scraper removes excess wax from surface of mold machine.

83

The crayons are then raised out of the holes.

The completed crayons are raised out of molds into holding tray.

A labeling machine individually wraps each crayon.

This machine puts a label on each crayon.

85

The labelled crayons are ready to be collated.

Different colored crayons are put in this machine.

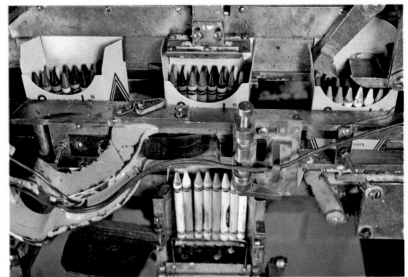

The packaging machines put crayons into boxes.

This machine puts the crayons in boxes.

Now the crayons are ready to use.

All workers do not make or grow goods.
Some workers do things for other people.
Workers who do things for others
provide, or give, <u>services</u>.
Your teacher provides a service.

This teacher is reading to the class.

88

meter reader

Ask: Do you think the boy and girl are earning money? How will they use the money they earn? (To buy wants and needs)

delivering newspapers

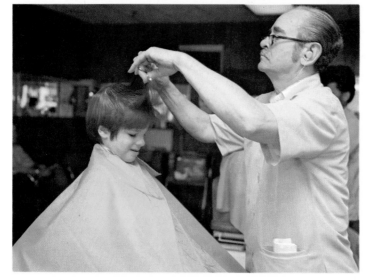

barber

A police officer provides a service.
Can you name some other workers
who provide a service?

police officer

89

silo for storing food for cows

dairy farm

    All workers cannot make goods.
All workers cannot give services.
People work together to provide
goods and services.
    This is a dairy farm.
It is outside a city.
Dairy farmers raise cows for milk.
The milk is sold to a milk-processing plant.

Ask pupils to name some other food made
from milk.

90

milking machines

Cows are milked
twice a day.

91

refrigerated truck

Raw milk is taken to a dairy plant for processing.

A truck comes to the farm to get the milk.
The driver of the truck takes the milk to the plant.

This is a special truck. It keeps the milk cold until it reaches the milk-processing plant.

Milk must undergo testing for quality and purity. Then it is pasteurized, homogenized, and packaged.

Workers at the plant process the milk.

Milk is taken from the plant to stores.

Workers in stores sell the milk.

Milk is one of the most important foods.
Many workers are needed to get milk
from the farm to your home.

Ask: Who are some workers that earn a living from milk? (Farmer, truck driver, worker at a milk-processing plant, salesperson in a store)

bank

teller

deposit slip

Lesson 7

Explain that long ago people could not buy goods and services. People built their own homes, grew and canned their own food, and made their own clothes. They also cut their own hair and did all their own work.

Today most people buy goods and services.

They must choose what goods and services to buy.

Sometimes people <u>save</u> money for what they want.

To save money means to put it away.

Explain that most people do not have enough money to buy all the goods and services they need. Sometimes they must save until they have enough money. Ask: Where do people save their money? Have you ever been to a bank? Now would be a good time to tell pupils some of the things that go on in a bank. If possible, show them a bankbook and a deposit slip.

96

Many people make a <u>budget</u>.
A budget is a spending plan.

Look at the pie graph.
It shows how one family budgets its money.
What is most of the money used for?
Why do they save some of their money?

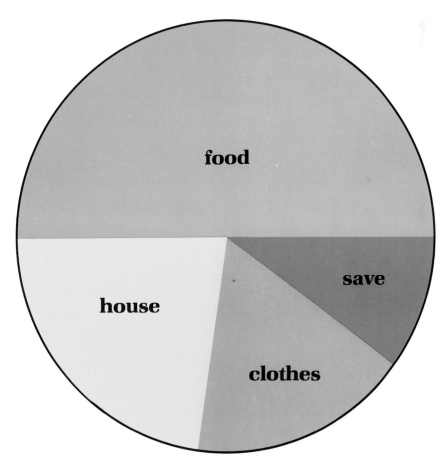

Ask: What does the graph show?

Our country has many workers.
They do many kinds of work.
They make and grow many kinds of goods.
They provide many kinds of services.
We are proud of our jobs and our workers.

A special day has been set aside
to honor workers in America.
It is called Labor Day.

Labor Day is celebrated on the
first Monday in September.
It is a holiday for workers.
There are picnics and parades.
It is a day of fun.

KEY FACTS

1. Food, clothes, and shelter are the three basic needs.

2. People do many different kinds of work.

3. The money people get for doing work is called income.

4. Income is used to buy wants and needs.

5. Labor Day is a holiday honoring workers in America.

VOCABULARY QUIZ

Number your paper from 1 to 6. Choose the right word for each sentence.

save   need

goods   budget

service   money

1. Things made or grown are called _____goods_____.

2. A spending plan is a _____budget_____.

3. Food is a _____need_____.

4. People work to earn _____money_____.

5. A police officer provides a _____service_____.

6. To _____save_____ money means to put it away.

REVIEW QUESTIONS

1. What is a need?

2. What is a want?

3. How do people earn money?

4. What do you call the money people earn for their work?

5. Name two service workers.

6. What holiday honors American workers?

7. In what month is Labor Day celebrated?

ACTIVITIES

1. Pretend you have earned a dollar. Make a pie graph showing how you would spend the dollar.

2. Make a picture showing a job that children can do to earn money.

3. Write a short poem about why people need friends.

Answers to review questions:
1. Something a person must have to live
2. Something a person would like to have but does not need
3. By working
4. Income
5. Answers will vary.
6. Labor Day
7. September

READING A GRAPH

A graph can tell us many things.
This graph tells what kinds of pets
are owned by the children on Elm Street.
Each child owns one pet.

Study the graph carefully.
Then answer the following questions.

1. What does the graph show?

2. How many children own birds?

3. What kind of pet is owned
by the most children?

4. Are there more rabbits than cats?

5. How many children own fish?

6. How many pets are on Elm Street?

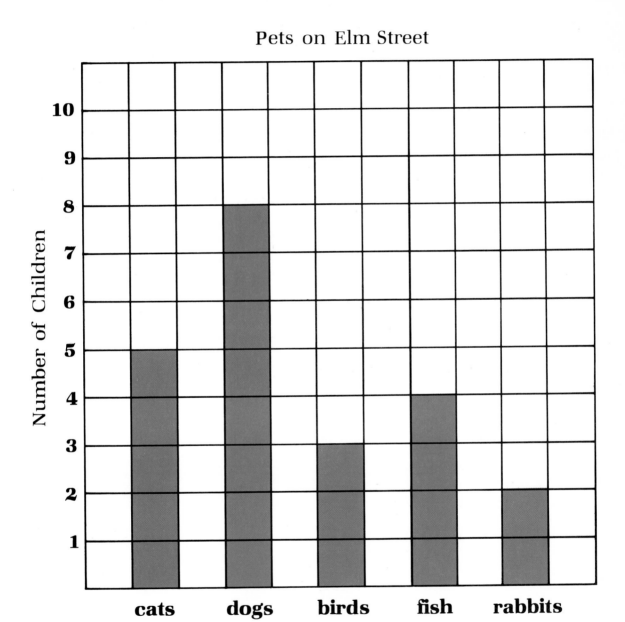

Pets on Elm Street

Suppose there were
No stop and go,
No taking turns,
No moving slow.

Suppose there were
No rules to say
"Keep to the right"
or "Go one way."

Suppose there were
No rules at all
For streets or parks
Or playing ball.

Do you think
No rules would be
The best for your
Community?

Call on pupils to read the poem.

a Little League game

Explain that a rule is something that tells people what to do and what not to do. Help pupils understand that they follow many rules each day. Ask: What time do you have to be in school? What time do you leave school? Can you go to school at any time during the day? Can you leave at any time? Do you think we need rules for going to and leaving school?

All people need rules to live by.

Rules help people get along with one another.

They make sure everyone is treated
in a fair way.

This picture shows what can happen
when people do not follow the rules.

Have the pupils study the picture and find some things that tell people what rules to follow. (Traffic light, signs) Have them point out some people who are not following the rules. Ask: Why do you think these rules are made? Are they good rules? What might happen if we did not have these rules? Would you want to cross this busy street if people did not obey traffic rules?

Now look at this picture.
What has changed?
Do rules help people?
Is it easier for everyone
when rules are followed?

Ask: What has changed in this picture? Are people following the traffic rules?

Community rules are sometimes shown on signs. The signs remind people of the rules of the community.

Look at the pictures on these pages. Do you know what these signs mean?

Discuss each sign. Ask: Have you seen signs like these in your community? Why do you think they are there? How do these signs help people? Why is it important to obey these rules?

Ask: Where is this family? Why, do you think, are they wearing life jackets? Do you think it is a good rule to wear a life jacket when you're in a boat? What are some other rules people should follow when they are in a boat?

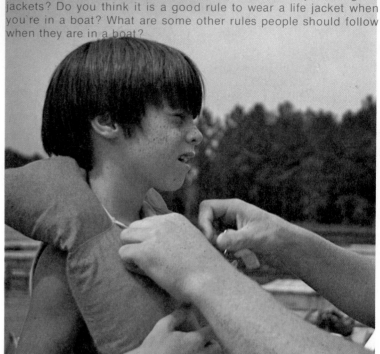

Families have rules.

Rules help families live better.

They help families stay safe and healthy.

Some families have rules

about eating and sleeping.

Some have rules for sharing the work.

What rules do these pictures show?

Which rule helps people stay safe?

Ask: Do you follow rules at home? Why, do you think, is the girl brushing her teeth? Do you have to brush your teeth? How often do you brush? Explain that some rules are to keep people safe and healthy.

Explain that rules can sometimes be broken. Ask: Do you always go to bed at the same time? Are there times when you can stay up later?

Ask: When you play games with your friends, how do you know who wins? Would it be fun to play a game if no one followed the rules? Emphasize that following the rules in a game makes sure everyone is treated in a fair way.

Schools have rules.

There are rules for playing.

There are rules for learning.

There are safety rules.

What rules do you follow in your school?

Ask: What rules do you have to follow in a library? This would be a good time to discuss rules of good manners.

Ask: Why do these pupils have their hands raised? What rule are they following? Is this a good rule to follow in school? What would happen if everyone talked at the same time?

Teachers help you learn to follow rules in a classroom.

Ask: Do you think it is important to know about fire safety rules? Read the fire drill rules to the class. Also, read the fire drill rules for your school.

Ask: Who helps you learn to follow rules in school? Do teachers have to follow rules?

Fire Drill Safety Rules

1. Form a line at the door.
2. Walk, don't run, to nearest exit
3. Be very quiet.

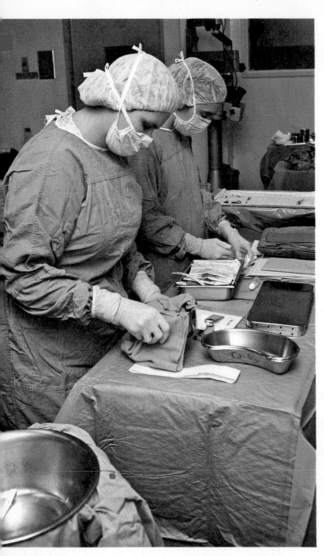

People who work follow rules.
Some rules help people work together.
Others help keep people safe and healthy.

Some jobs have special rules.
Special rules help protect workers.
What would happen if this worker
did not follow the rules?

Point out that some rules can be broken. Some cannot. Laws are rules that people must obey. Ask: Do you know what happens when people disobey laws?

People in towns and cities have rules.

These rules are called laws.

Laws are rules that people must obey.

Laws help protect the rights of people.

They help protect property.

People help their community when they obey laws.

Citizens in a community pick leaders.
The citizens vote for the people they want.
The people who get the most votes are elected.

Leaders help make the plans and laws
for a community.
Most towns and cities have a mayor.
The mayor helps the community
make and keep its laws.

Families pay money to the community.
The money is called taxes.
This money pays for community services.

Many people work for a community.
The community pays these workers
with the money from taxes.
Community workers help make the community
a better place to live.

The governor of Tennessee works in this building.

There are many towns and cities in a state.
One town or city cannot make plans
and laws for others.
Leaders are elected to help make plans
and laws for the state.
Each state has a leader called the <u>governor</u>.
The governor is elected by the people of the state.

The governor works at the state capital. Each state
capital has a special building called the Capitol.

Each state has a <u>capital city</u>.
Laws and plans for the state
are made in the capital city.

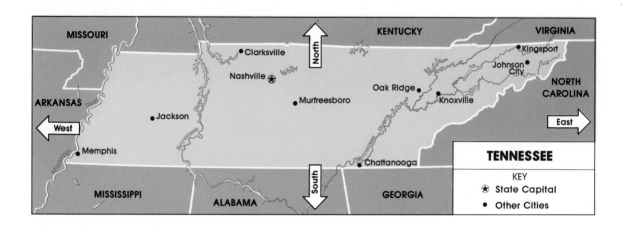

The map shows the state of Tennessee.
Nashville is the capital of Tennessee.
The governor and other state leaders
of Tennessee work in Nashville.
Find Nashville on the map.

Explain that a state's capital city is a city where the leaders of the state meet.
Have pupils find the symbol in the map key that stands for a state capital.

Ask: How does the map key help you identify the state capital of Tennessee?

The United States has 50 states.
These states make up our country.

Ask: How many states are in our country? Does each state
have a capital city? What is the capital city of your state?

122

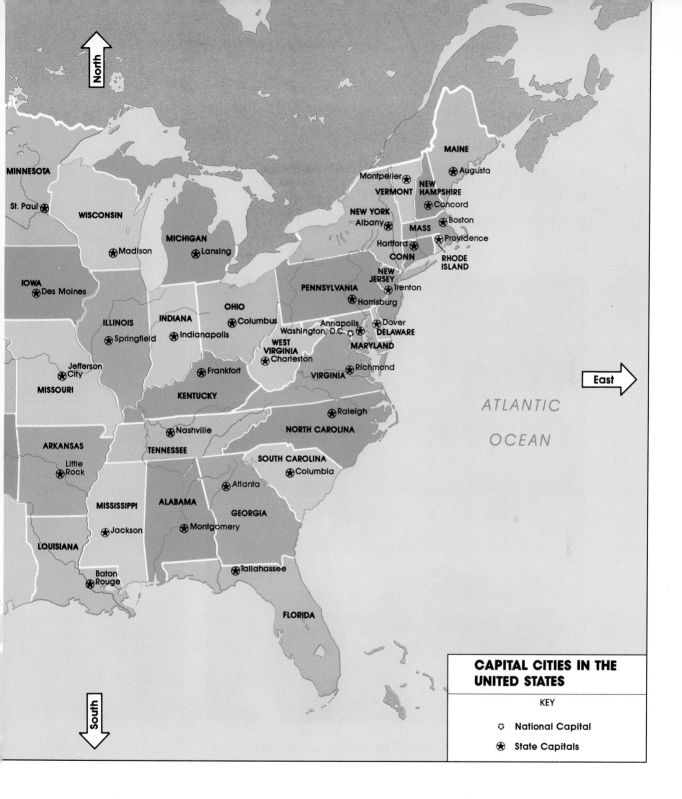

The map shows each state capital.
Do you know the capital of your state?

One state cannot plan and make laws
for another. But they work together
to make some plans and laws.
The people in each state pick leaders
to be members of Congress.
Congress helps make plans and laws
for all the states.

Our country has one special leader.
This leader is the President.
The people of the United States
elect the President.
The President helps to make plans and laws
for all the people.

124

Aerial view of Washington, D.C.

Many of the leaders in our country
work in Washington, D.C. This city is a capital,
but it is not one of the 50 state capitals.
Washington, D.C., is our national capital.
The President lives and works in Washington, D.C.

125

KEY FACTS

1. People need rules to live by.
2. Rules help keep people safe and healthy.
3. Laws are rules that must be obeyed.
4. Laws help protect people's rights and property.
5. Leaders are elected to make laws and plans.
6. Families pay taxes to the community.
7. The community uses taxes to buy goods and services.
8. Each state has a capital city.
9. The President is the leader of our country.
10. Our national capital is Washington, D.C.

VOCABULARY QUIZ

Number your paper from 1 to 6.

Choose the right ending for each sentence.

elected	mayor
President	taxes
voting	governor

1. The money families pay to a community is called ____taxes____.
2. People pick their leaders by ____voting____.
3. The people who get the most votes are ____elected____.
4. The leader of a town or city is the ____mayor____.
5. The leader of a state is the ____governor____.
6. The leader of our country is the ____President____.

REVIEW QUESTIONS

1. Name two rules you observe at home.

2. Who helps you follow classroom rules?

3. What are laws?

4. What are taxes used for?

5. How many states are in the United States?

6. Who is the leader of our country?

7. What is the name of our national capital?

ACTIVITIES

1. Find pictures showing some services in your community that are paid for with money from taxes.

2. Make up a rule for your class. Make a sign showing the rule.

3. Find out who the leaders of your community are and where they meet.

Answers to Review Questions:

1. Answers will vary.
2. Teacher
3. Rules
4. To pay for community goods and services
5. Fifty
6. President
7. Washington, D.C.

IDENTIFYING STATES

States come in different shapes and sizes.
Some state are large. Some are small.
These outline maps show some states in the
United States. Use the map on pages 122 – 123
to identify the states.

On a separate sheet of paper, write
the name of the states. Beside the name
of each state, write the name of its capital city.

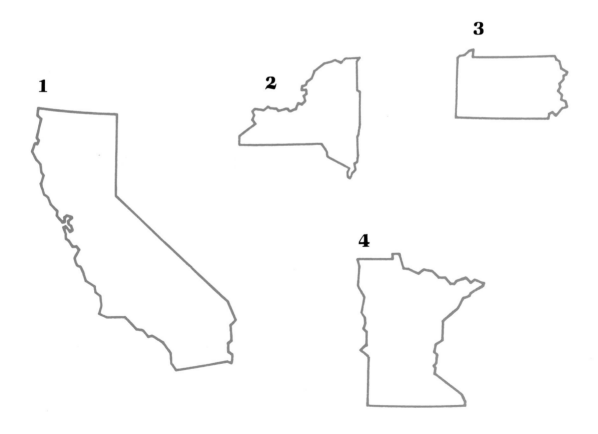

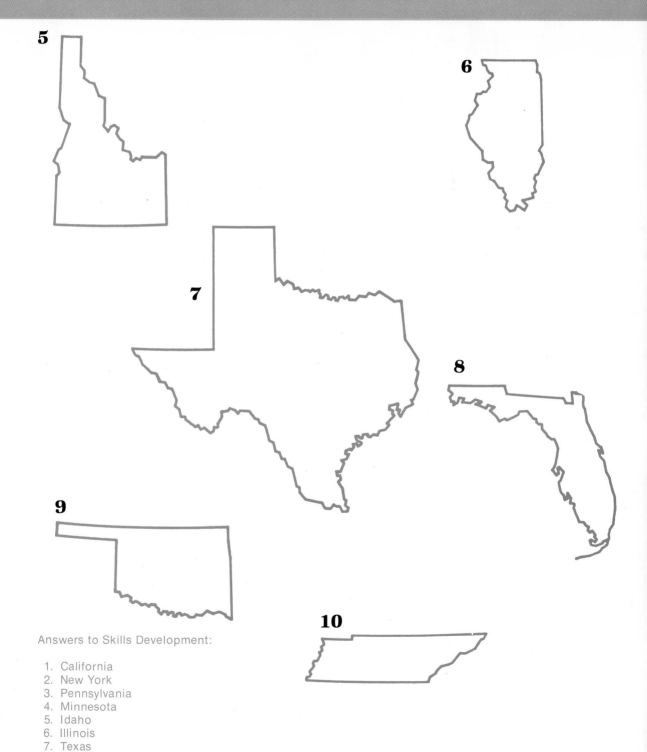

5

6

7

8

9

10

Answers to Skills Development:

1. California
2. New York
3. Pennsylvania
4. Minnesota
5. Idaho
6. Illinois
7. Texas
8. Florida
9. Oklahoma
10. Tennessee

CHAPTER 5

Communities Long Ago and Today

Have you ever been to a community
That was started a long time ago?
Have you walked on streets made of brick
Or seen candle-lit windows aglow?

Do you wonder how people lived then—
What they ate, how they worked, how they played?
Do you think the children had cookies
Or knew how to make lemonade?

Do you think you'd like to live in
A community from long, long ago?
Why don't you choose one to visit?
Then, perhaps, you will know.

Call on pupils to read the poem.

a street in Colonial Williamsburg
restoration, Williamsburg, Virginia

bow and arrow

canoe

Our country has not always been divided
into 50 states. The first states became states
about 200 years ago.

The story of our country from its beginnings
up to today is called our country's history.
Today there are towns and cities.
But it has not always been this way.

mountains

Long ago what is now the United States
was a large <u>wilderness</u>.

Many years ago there were no towns or cities.
There were no stores or factories.
There were no schools or highways.
But there were people living here.
They were the first Americans.
Today we call them Indians or Native Americans.

The Indians were the first people
to live in our country.

Explain that wigwams were made of young green trees covered with birchbark strips. A wigwam could be built in one day.

The Indians lived in groups called tribes.
A tribe was made up of many families.
They lived in small communities called <u>villages</u>.

   All tribes were not the same.
They had different names and
different ways of doing things.
They built different kinds of houses.

   Some tribes built round houses
called wigwams.

This man is going off into the forest to hunt.

Some pueblos were five stories tall. Outside ladders were used to reach the upper floors.

Some built apartment buildings called pueblos.

Some built cone-shaped houses called tepees.

Tell pupils that some tepees were covered with animal skins or fur. Some were covered with rush mats.

A longhouse was large enough for several families to live in at the same time.

Explain that the houses on pp. 134–137 are just a few of the many kinds of houses build by Native Americans.

The Iroquois Indians built longhouses.
The longhouses were built in a circle.
A tall fence was built around the village.
The fence gave protection to the village.
The Iroquois hunted in the forests.
They fished in the lakes and rivers.
They planted corn, beans, and squash.

136

Indian families made their clothing
from animal skins. Sometimes they traded
with other tribes. But most Indian families
did not depend on others.
They did everything for themselves.

Explain that many explorers had come to America long before the first colonists left England.

Over 350 years ago some people
left their homes in England.
They crossed the Atlantic Ocean to America.
These people were called colonists. They were also called settlers.
They came to our country to find a new home.
The colonists started a <u>settlement</u>.
A settlement is a small community.
They named their settlement Jamestown,
after King James of England. The colonists reached Jamestown, Virginia, in 1607.
Jamestown was built in a part of America
called Virginia. Jamestown is the oldest
English settlement in our country.

Explain that the colonists from England were not the first people to start settlements in America. Spanish settlers came long before the English. St. Augustine in Florida was started in 1565. It is the oldest city in America.

Fort James · wooden houses · water

One of the first things the colonists did
was to build a fort along the James River.
A fort is a strong building.
It gave protection to the colonists.

Ask: What do you think the colonists needed protection from?

They also built log cabins.

Most log cabins were one-room houses.

Soon stores and other buildings were built.

The settlement of Jamestown began to grow.

The second oldest English settlement
is Plymouth. The colonists built Plymouth
in what is now the state of Massachusetts.
Their Indian neighbors taught them farming skills.
The Indians taught the colonists
how to grow beans, corn, and squash.
These foods helped the colonists survive
the long, cold winter.

The colonists were thankful for their new home.
They invited the Indians to a celebration.
The Indians and colonists played games
and cooked a big dinner. This celebration
was the first Thanksgiving in our country.
Today Thanksgiving is still celebrated.

The first Thanksgiving was the beginning of an American tradition of
giving thanks for our homes, our families, and our friends.

The celebration lasted three days.

Tell pupils that the Pilgrims and Indians ate outside at a long table.
Some of the things they ate were corn, beans, pumpkins, squash,
clams, turkey, duck, and deer meat.

teacher

Pupils learned reading, writing, and arithmetic.

Jamestown and Plymouth were the first
two English settlements in our country.
Soon many other settlements were built.
People began doing special kinds of work.
Many were still farmers.
But others became teachers, carpenters, and
tinsmiths.
Families no longer did everything for themselves.

144

tinsmith

carpenter

145

Families today have many kinds of communities to live in.
There are rural communities and suburbs.
There are small towns and large cities.

Long ago people made their own clothes.
Today we can buy our clothes in stores.
Long ago people farmed and hunted for food.
Today there are supermarkets and grocery stores.

People used to make their homes from trees and mud. Now homes are made of wood, brick, and many other things.

Ask: How is this street of long ago different from the picture on the next page? What things have changed?

People used to travel in canoes and wagons.
Today there are cars, trains, and airplanes.
People long ago spent most of their time
meeting their basic needs.
Today machines do much of the work.
Families have more time for fun.

Life today is different from life in
Indian villages and colonist settlements.
Can you name some other ways
communities have changed?

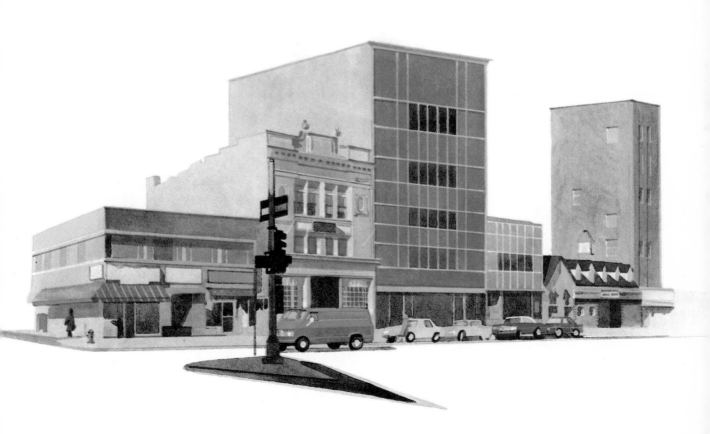

The people who settled in Jamestown and Plymouth were from England.

After these colonists, other people came to America. They came from countries in Africa and Asia. They came from countries in Europe and from Australia. They came from countries in South America and from countries in other parts of North America.

People from all over the world came to live in the United States. These people brought different ways of living to America. They ate different foods. They dressed differently. They had different ways of doing things.

148

149

Today our country is made up
of people of different backgrounds.
Some families are very much like yours.
Other families may seem very different.
Yet all are Americans.
All have given something
to our communities and our nation.
All have helped to make our nation
a better place in which to live.

KEY FACTS

1. Long ago America was a large wilderness.

2. The Indians were the first people to live in this country.

3. The colonists came to American to find a new home.

4. Jamestown was the first English settlement in America.

5. The colonists and the Indians celebrated the first Thanksgiving.

6. Today the United States is made up of people from all over the world.

VOCABULARY QUIZ

Number your paper from 1 to 6. Write the word that completes each sentence.

| log cabins | villages | canoes |
| Plymouth | Jamestown | wigwams |

1. Indian families lived in communities called ___villages___.

2. The first English settlement in America was ___Jamestown___.

3. The colonists built houses called ___log cabins___.

4. Long ago people traveled in wagons and ___canoes___.

5. ___Plymouth___ was the second English settlement in America.

6. Some Indian tribes built round houses called ___wigwams___.

REVIEW QUESTIONS

1. Who were the first Americans? Indians or Native Americans
2. What ocean did the colonists cross to reach America? Atlantic Ocean
3. In what part of America was Jamestown built? Virginia
4. Why did the colonists built a fort? to protect themselves
5. How did the Indians help the colonists? Answers will vary

ACTIVITIES

1. Pretend you and your family came to
America with the first colonists.
Draw a picture of the settlement
you would have lived in.
2. Find a picture showing something
the colonists had to do for themselves.
Tell how it is done today.

MAPPING A PICTURE

Jamestown was the first English settlement in America.

The picture on the next page shows how Jamestown looked a long time ago.

Draw a map of this picture.
Add a key to the map. Make up symbols to stand for things in the picture.
Some things you may want to show water, trees, houses, and boats.

Beside each symbol write what it stands for.

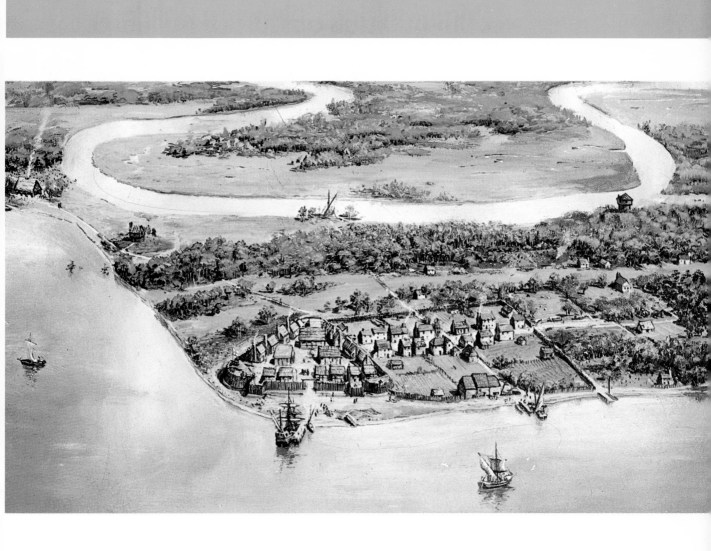

How we love to celebrate
To see a band passing by,
To hear a choir singing
Or fireworks lighting the sky.

How we love to celebrate
At all times of the year,
Sometimes at noisy fairgrounds,
Sometimes with family near.

How we love to celebrate
On occasions big and small!
We have some wonderful holidays—
Let's celebrate them all!

Call on pupils to read the poem. Ask them to tell what is going on in the picture.

fireworks celebrating our country's 200th birthday

156

Americans celebrate many special days.
Some are birthdays.
Some are days important things happened.

These boys and girls are having a party.
They are celebrating a special day.
Do you know what special day it is?
It is a birthday.

Explain that a birthday is a very special day. Refer to the classroom calendar graph made in the Getting Started activity. Ask: Whose birthday is next on the calendar? What is the date of that person's birthday? On what day is it?

You have a birthday.
It is your special day.
Your birthday is the day you were born.
Each birthday you are a year older.
When is your birthday?

Long ago a man left his home across the ocean.
He sailed to America.
His name was Christopher Columbus.
When Columbus returned home,
he told about the new land he had seen.
People wanted to see this new land.
Soon more people **sailed** to America.

Columbus and his crew sailed from Spain in three small ships. The ships were named the *Niña*, the *Pinta*, and the *Santa María*.

We remember Columbus on the second Monday in October.

Many towns and cities in America are named for Columbus.

Columbus first landed in North America in 1492.

Veterans are people who have served
in the armed forces.
We are proud of the people
who have fought for our country.

To honor our veterans, we celebrate
Veterans Day on November 11.
Most towns and cities have parades.
Veterans dress in their uniforms.
They march in the parades.

Thanksgiving Day was started by the Pilgrims.
The Pilgrims were a group of colonists
who came to America.
  Indians living in America
taught the Pilgrims how to grow food.
They taught them to fish and hunt, too.

The pilgrims were thankful for their new home
and new friends. They were thankful for their food.
The Pilgrims decided to have a big feast.
They invited the Indians.

Have pupils compare Thanksgiving today with
the first Thanksgiving.

This was the first Thanksgiving.

164

Tell pupils that the first Thanksgiving was held in the early fall of 1621. The
Pilgrims decided to hold a feast to give thanks for their harvest, their health,
and their friendship with the Indians. Explain that a harvest is a time when
crops are picked or gathered.

Thanksgiving Day is very special to Americans.
We remember the Pilgrims and the Indians.
We are thankful for the things we have.
    Each year we celebrate Thanksgiving
on the fourth Thursday in November.

Point out that many cities and towns have a parade on Thanksgiving Day. This picture
shows a Thanksgiving Day parade in New York City.

165

Martin Luther King, Jr., was born
on January 15, 1929.

King was born in Atlanta, Georgia.

Explain that King was a civil rights leader. Civil rights are the freedoms and rights to which citizens of a community, state, or nation are entitled. You might want to discuss with the class some of the rights mentioned in the Bill of Rights.

In 1964 King was awarded the Nobel Peace Prize.

As a young man he had a dream.
He dreamed of a better life for all Americans.
He wanted people to live together in peace.

King worked hard to make his dream come true.
We remember him on his birthday every year.

King died in 1968. Many cities and towns have a parade on his birthday.

Abraham Lincoln was born on February 12, 1809.

Explain that after working on the farm all day, Lincoln would read law books at night. He attended school only when he could be spared from working on the farm.

As a boy, Lincoln helped on his family's farm.
He went to school for only a few years.
He taught himself to read law books.

Lincoln was the 16th President of the United States.
We celebrate his birthday every year.

Explain that George Washington was a general in the American army. He led the American soldiers against the soldiers of England.

George Washington was born on February 22, 1732.

We celebrate his birthday on the third Monday in February. Washington was the first President of the United States.

This is the house where Washington lived.

Washington and his family lived on a large farm in Virginia called Mount Vernon. Today Mount Vernon is a historic site. Tourists from all over the world visit it each year.

Memorial Day is celebrated in May.
It is a day we honor those who died
for our country.
Services and programs help us to remember
these people.
A special service is held
at the Tomb of the Unknown Soldier.

People also remember family and friends
who are no longer living.

Many years ago our country had only 13 states.

The people living in those states had been ruled by a king in England. England is a country in Europe. The king made laws for Americans to obey. The Americans would not obey the laws. They wanted to change them.

England and the Americans fought a war. The Americans won the war. They won their freedom from England.

On July 4, 1776, the Americans had a celebration. It was a birthday party for our country. They called the celebration Independence Day.

This painting is called "The Spirit of '76." It shows a fife player and two drummers leading American soldiers into battle.

After the war the United States grew.
Today there are 50 states.
The American flag is our country's symbol.
Each star in our flag stands for a state.
The flag has 13 stripes.
Each stripe stands for one
of the first 13 states.
Every July 4, Americans celebrate
Independence Day.
Flags hang from homes and buildings.
We are proud of our freedom.
We are proud to be Americans.

175

KEY FACTS

1. Everyone has a birthday once a year.
2. Holidays honor important people or events.
3. Columbus was one of the first people to sail to America.
4. Veterans are people who have served in the armed forces.
5. George Washington was the first President of the United States.
6. July 4 is the birthday of our country.
7. The American flag is a symbol of our country.

VOCABULARY QUIZ

Number your paper from 1 to 6.
Write T if the sentence is true.
Write F is the sentence is false.

1. Christopher Columbus started Thanksgiving Day. false
2. George Washington was the first President of our country. true
3. Memorial Day is celebrated in December. false
4. Today our country has 50 states. true
5. The flag is a symbol of our country. true
6. Independence Day is our country's birthday. true

REVIEW QUESTIONS

1. What is the name of the day you were born?
2. In what month is Columbus Day celebrated?
3. Who was the first President of our country?
4. What do we call our country's birthday?
5. How many stars are in our flag?
6. What do the stars stand for?
7. How many stripes are in our flag?
8. What do the stripes stand for?

ACTIVITIES

1. Find some pictures of presidents of our country.
2. Draw and color a picture of the American flag.
3. Find some pictures of other holidays Americans celebrate.

Answers to Review Questions:
1. Answers will vary.
2. October
3. George Washington
4. Independence Day or the Fourth of July
5. Fifty
6. The fifty states (one for each state)
7. Thirteen
8. The first thirteen states

READING A CALENDAR

A calendar shows many things.

It shows the months in the year.

It shows the weeks in a month.

It shows the days in a week.

A calendar also shows when a holiday or
event should be celebrated.

This is the calendar for 1984.
Study it carefully and answer the following questions.

1. How many days are there in a week?

2. What day of the week is May 3?

3. The first **S** stands for Sunday.
What do the other letters stand for?

4. Which day comes first in the
week, Wednesday or Thursday?

5. What is the first month of the year?

6. How many days are in the month of December?

7. Thanksgiving Day is November 22.
What day of the week is November 22?

JANUARY

S	M	T	W	T	F	S
1	2	3	4	5	6	7
8	9	10	11	12	13	14
15	16	17	18	19	20	21
22	23	24	25	26	27	28
29	30	31				

FEBRUARY

S	M	T	W	T	F	S
			1	2	3	4
5	6	7	8	9	10	11
12	13	14	15	16	17	18
19	20	21	22	23	24	25
26	27	28	29			

MARCH

S	M	T	W	T	F	S
				1	2	3
4	5	6	7	8	9	10
11	12	13	14	15	16	17
18	19	20	21	22	23	24
25	26	27	28	29	30	31

APRIL

S	M	T	W	T	F	S
1	2	3	4	5	6	7
8	9	10	11	12	13	14
15	16	17	18	19	20	21
22	23	24	25	26	27	28
29	30					

MAY

S	M	T	W	T	F	S
		1	2	3	4	5
6	7	8	9	10	11	12
13	14	15	16	17	18	19
20	21	22	23	24	25	26
27	28	29	30	31		

JUNE

S	M	T	W	T	F	S
					1	2
3	4	5	6	7	8	9
10	11	12	13	14	15	16
17	18	19	20	21	22	23
24	25	26	27	28	29	30

JULY

S	M	T	W	T	F	S
1	2	3	4	5	6	7
8	9	10	11	12	13	14
15	16	17	18	19	20	21
22	23	24	25	26	27	28
29	30	31				

AUGUST

S	M	T	W	T	F	S
			1	2	3	4
5	6	7	8	9	10	11
12	13	14	15	16	17	18
19	20	21	22	23	24	25
26	27	28	29	30	31	

SEPTEMBER

S	M	T	W	T	F	S
						1
2	3	4	5	6	7	8
9	10	11	12	13	14	15
16	17	18	19	20	21	22
23	24	25	26	27	28	29
30						

OCTOBER

S	M	T	W	T	F	S
	1	2	3	4	5	6
7	8	9	10	11	12	13
14	15	16	17	18	19	20
21	22	23	24	25	26	27
28	29	30	31			

NOVEMBER

S	M	T	W	T	F	S
				1	2	3
4	5	6	7	8	9	10
11	12	13	14	15	16	17
18	19	20	21	22	23	24
25	26	27	28	29	30	

DECEMBER

S	M	T	W	T	F	S
						1
2	3	4	5	6	7	8
9	10	11	12	13	14	15
16	17	18	19	20	21	22
23	24	25	26	27	28	29
30	31					

GLOSSARY

The page numbers tell where each word first appears in the text.

apartment building. A building that has separate homes for many families. p. 44.

budget. A spending plan to help people decide how to use their money. p. 97.

capital city. The city where leaders of a country or state meet and work. p. 121.

citizen. A person who is a member of a community, state or country. p. 46.

city. A large community where many people live and work. p.58.

community. People or families who live in a certain area or place. p. 33.

Congress. The men and women chosen to help make laws for all the people in our country. p. 124.

continent. One of the seven large bodies of land on the earth. The continents are North America, South America, Europe, Asia, Africa, Australia, and Antarctica. p. 22.

country. A large area of land and the people who live there. The United States is your country. p. 25.

direction. A way in which a person or thing faces, points, or moves. p. 16.

earth. The planet on which we live. The earth is made up of land and water. p. 2.

east. The direction from which the sun seems to rise each morning. East is the direction to your right when you face north. p. 20.

elect. To choose leaders by voting. Citizens of a state or country elect leaders to help make plans and laws. p. 118.

explorers. People who look for new places. p. 18.

factory. A place where goods are made. p. 59.

globe. A small model of the earth. p. 15.

goods. Things that are made and sold. Foods and clothes are goods. p. 51.

governor. A person who is elected by the people of a state to be their leader. Each state in our country has a governor. p. 120.

hill. A raised part of the land. p. 7.

houseboat. A house on water. p. 45.

house trailer. A house that can be moved from place to place. p. 45.

income. The money people earn for the work they do. Income is used to buy wants and needs. p. 80.

island. A body of land that has water all around it. p. 10.

lake. A body of water with land all around it. p. 9.

law. A rule that people must obey. p. 116.

map. A flat drawing of the earth or part of the earth. p. 12.

model. A small-scale representation of an object. A globe is a model of the earth. p. 15

mountain. Very high land. Mountains are higher than hills. p. 7.

museum. A building where interesting objects are collected and displayed. p. 56.

needs. Things that all people must have to live. Three basic needs are food, clothes, and shelter. p. 74.

neighborhood. A small part of a community in a town or city. p. 42.

neighbors. People or families who live near one another. p. 42.

north. The direction toward the North Pole. p. 16.

North Pole. The place on earth that is farthest north. p. 16.

ocean. A large body of salt water. p. 8.

opposite. Facing, in front of, or across from. The North Pole is opposite the South Pole. p. 17.

peninsula. A piece of land that has water nearly all around it. A peninsula is part of a larger body of land. p. 10.

plain. A level area of land. p. 6.

President. The leader of our country. p. 124.

river. A large stream of water that flows through the land. p. 9.

rural community. A community with few people and a lot of land. p. 62.

save. To put away for later use. p. 96.

services. Kinds of work other than making goods. p. 54.

settlement. A small community. p. 140.

south. The direction toward the South Pole. p. 17.

South Pole. The place on earth that is farthest south. p. 17.

state. One of the 50 parts of the United States. p. 26.

suburb. A city or town near a large city. p. 60.

taxes. Money people and families pay to their government. Taxes pay for community goods and services. p. 119.

town. A small community with few homes and stores. p. 63.

transportation. The movement of people and goods from one place to another. p. 61.

typewriter. A machine that prints letters on paper. p. 58.

village. A very small community. A village is smaller than a town. p. 134.

wants. Things that people like to have but do not need. p. 74.

west. The direction toward which the sun seems to set at night. p. 20.

wilderness. An area of land that has not been changed by people. p. 133.

INDEX

CREDITS

Cover: Gregory Hergert
Graphs and Charts: Joe LeMonnier/Craven Design Studio, Inc.
Maps: R.R. Donnelley Cartographic Services

Chapter 1 1: Fritz Prenzel/Bruce Coleman. 2–3: Lester Tinker/Taurus Photos. 3: © Harald Sund. 4: *t.* Summer Productions/Taurus Photos; *b.* John Running. 5: Carolyn Croll. 6–7: Cary Wolinsky/Stock, Boston. 7: *t.* © Harald Sund; *b.* Jen & Des Bartlett/Bruce Coleman. 8: Frederick Bodin/Stock, Boston. 9: *t.* Harald Sund; *b.* Cary Wolinsky/Stock, Boston. 10: *t.* Nicholas DeVore III/Bruce Coleman; *b.* © Harald Sund. 11: Herman Vestal. 12: Silver Burdett, courtesy of NORTHEAST AIRWAYS. 14: NASA. 15, 16, 17: Imagery. 18: *t.* The Bettmann Archive; *b.l., b.r.* Culver Pictures. 19: *t.* © 1982 C. Bonnington/Woodfin Camp & Associates; *b.* Courtesy, U.S. Coast Guard. 21: Maggie Swanson. 25: *t.* Mulvey-Crump Associates; *b.* © R. Rowan/Photo Researchers, Inc.; 28: © Lee Battaglia/Photo Researchers, Inc. 31: *t.l.* © Russ Kinne/Photo Researchers, Inc.; *t.r.* M. Timothy O'Keefe/Bruce Coleman; *m.l.* Wm. R. Wright/Taurus Photos; *m.r.* Courtesy, LION COUNTRY SAFARI, INC., Florida; *b.l.* J. Gerard Smith; *b.r.* © George Gerster/Photo Researchers, Inc. 32: *l.* H.A. Thornhill, National Audubon Society photograph/Photo Researchers, Inc.; *b.r.* R.E. Pelham/Bruce Coleman. 33: *t.* J. Messerschmidt/Bruce Coleman; *b.* Peter Vandermark/Stock, Boston. 37: Maggie Swanson.

Chapter 2 38–39: R. Thompson/Taurus Photos. 40: Eric Carle/Shostal Associates. 40–41: *t.* Dr. E.R. Degginger; *b.* Harvey Lloyd/Peter Arnold, Inc. 41: Voscar/Shostal Associates. 42: Pam Hasegawa. 42–43: Eric Anderson/Stock, Boston. 43: Cliff Wallace/Taurus Photos. 44: *t.* Silver Burdett; *b.* Vance Henry/Taurus Photos. 45: *t.* © Michael Philip Manheim/Photo Researchers, Inc.; *m.* Eric Carle/Shostal Associates; *b.* Wm. B. Finch/Stock, Boston. 46: Frank Siteman/Stock, Boston. 47: *t.* Richard Choy/Peter Arnold, Inc.; *b.* Silver Burdett. 48: Silver Burdett. 49: *t.* Bohdan Hrynewych/Stock, Boston; *b.* Imagery. 50: Silver Burdett. 51: Silver Burdett, courtesy, Quiet Cycles Ltd., Bernardsville, N.J. 52: Robert Weinreb/Bruce Coleman. 53: *t.* Silver Burdett; *b.* Courtesy, The Seeing Eye, Inc., Morristown, N.J. 54: *t.* Donald Dietz/Stock, Boston; *m.* Karen Collidge/Taurus Photos; *b.* Mark Mittleman/Taurus Photos. 55: *t.* John Running; *b.* J. Gerard Smith. 56: *t.* George Malave/Stock, Boston; *b.* Courtesy, Alabama Space and Rocket Center. 57: *L.* Foster/Bruce Coleman. 58–59: Michael Melford/Peter Arnold, Inc. 59: *l.* Silver Burdett; *r.* Cary Wolinsky/Stock, Boston. 60: Eric Carle/Shostal Associates. 60–61: Frank Wing/Stock, Boston. 62–63: Dr. E.R. Degginger. 66–67: © Harald Sund. 67: Cecile Brunswick/Peter Arnold, Inc.

Chapter 3 72–73: Paul Fusco/Magnum. 74–77: Silver Burdett. 78: *t.* Edward Lettau/Peter Arnold, Inc.; *b.* Pam Hasegawa. 79: John Running. 80: *t.* © Paolo Koch/Photo Researchers, Inc.; *m.* Silver Burdett; *b.* © 1982 Jeffrey Foxx/Woodfin Camp & Associates. 81: *t.* © Bruce Roberts/Photo Researchers, Inc. *b.* Owen Franken/Stock, Boston. 82–87: Michal Heron. 88: © Bruce Roberts/Photo Researchers, Inc. 89: *t.l.* Pam Hasegawa; *t.r.* Bob Roberts/Shostal Associates; *m.* John Clark/Shostal Associates; *b.* © Edward Lettau/Photo Researchers, Inc. 90–91: Richard Weiss/Peter Arnold, Inc. 91: © 1982 Sylvia Johnson/Woodfin Camp & Associates. 92: *t.* Alvin Upitis/Shostal Associates; *b.* © Joe Munroe/Photo Researchers, Inc. 93: Andre Abecassis/Visualeyes. 94: Silver Burdett, courtesy, New Village Market, New Vernon, N.J. 95: Silver Burdett. 96: Silver Burdett, courtesy, The Heritage Bank North, Morristown, N.J. 99: John Dyess.

Chapter 4 104–105: Elliot Erwitt/Magnum. 106–107: John Kilgrew. 108–109: Silver Burdett. 109: *b.* Marjorie Pickens for Silver Burdett. 110: Silver Burdett. 110–111: © Southern Living/Photo Researchers, Inc. 111: Silver Burdett. 112: *t.* Steve R. Scheerer/Taurus Photos; *b.* Elizabeth Crews/Stock, Boston. 113: *t.* © Roger Clark, Jr./Photo Researchers, Inc.; *b.* Silver Burdett. 114: *l.* © Russ Kinne/Photo Researchers, Inc.; *r.* A. D'Arazien/Shostal Associates. 115: Dr. E.R. Degginger. 116: Silver Burdett. 117: Cary Wolinsky/Stock, Boston. 118: *t.* Eric Carle/Shostal Associates; *b.* © Bruce Roberts/Photo Researchers, Inc. 119: Silver Burdett. 120: Courtesy, Dept. of Tourist Development, State of Tennessee. 124: © Allen Green/Photo Researchers, Inc. 124–125: M.E. Browning/Shostal Associates. 128–129: Pat Traub.

Chapter 5 130–131: Colonial Williamsburg Photograph. 132–147: Bill Schmidt. 148: J. Gerard Smith. 148–149: Harvey Lloyd/Peter Arnold, Inc. 149: *t.r.* Katrina Thomas/Photo Researchers, Inc.; *b.l.* Porges/Peter Arnold, Inc.; *b.r.* Mike Mazzaschi/Stock, Boston. 150: *t., b.l.* Eric Carle/Shostal Associates; *b.r.* L.L.T. Rhodes/Taurus Photos. 150–151: Eric Carle/Shostal Associates. 151: *t.r.* © 1982 C. Bonnington/Woodfin Camp & Associates; *m.* Beth Irwin/Taurus Photos; *b.l.* John Running; *b.r.* Werner Stoy/Camera Hawaii. 155: National Park Service, Jamestown.

Chapter 6 156–157: © George Holton/Photo Researchers, Inc. 158–159: Silver Burdett. 161: *t.* Courtesy of the U.S. Naval Academy Museum/Photo by M.E. Warren for Silver Burdett; *b.* Culver Pictures. 162: Eric Carle/Shostal Associates. 163: *t.* Martin Rotker/Taurus Photos; *b.* Gerhard Gscheidle/Peter Arnold, Inc. 164: Herman Vestal. 165: *t.* Augusts Upitis/Shostal Associates; *b.* 1982 Sepp Seitz/Woodfin Camp & Associates; *m.* Beth Irwin/Taurus Photos. 166: Ray C. Moore/Shostal Associates. 167: Eric Carle/Shostal Associates. 168: *t.l.* Brown Brothers; *b.l.* Culver Pictures; *r.* The Bettmann Archive. 169: © Goldman/Photo Researchers, Inc. 170: Brown Brothers. 171: *t.* "Battle of Trenton," Life Magazine, © 1950 Time Inc., courtesy, Authenticolor, and Kenneth M. Newman, The Old Print Shop, N.Y.C.; *b.* © Southern Living/Photo Researchers, Inc. 172: Charles May/Shostal Associates. 173: *t.* James H. Karales/Peter Arnold, Inc.; *b.* Richard Wood/Taurus Photos. 174: The original of this painting hangs in the Selectman's Room, Abbot Hall, Marblehead, Massachusetts. 175: *t.* McCarthy/Peter Arnold, Inc.; *b.* Owen Franken/Stock, Boston.

1 2 3 4 5 6 7 8 9 10—RRD—89 88 87 86 85 84 83 82 81

CHAPTER 1

Where We Live

CHAPTER 1

WHERE WE LIVE

Dear Parent,

I am pleased to inform you that during this school year we will be using the Silver Burdett social studies textbook titled *Neighborhoods and Communities.*

Your child will be learning about people in neighborhoods and communities in our country and around the world. I would like to involve you in our studies by means of parent letters. As we begin each chapter in the book, I will send you a letter to help keep you informed and to offer suggestions for ways you can help at home.

Our first chapter is called "Where We Live." It is about the earth and the people who live on the earth. Your child will learn about the earth through the use of some basic map and globe skills. In addition, your child will learn about natural features, such as oceans, mountains, islands, lakes, and rivers.

If you have old magazines, help your child find pictures of some natural features to bring to class. Play direction games to help reinforce your child's understanding of east, west, north, and south.

I am looking forward to an enjoyable year working with your child.

Sincerely,

CHAPTER 1 PAGES 1–37

WHERE WE LIVE

THEME

The earth is the home of all people. People live in different places on the earth.

OVERVIEW

In this chapter pupils learn about the earth they live on. They study the different landforms and bodies of water of the earth. A globe and maps are introduced as symbols that represent the earth. By using a globe and a variety of maps, pupils develop important understandings about the earth and learn skills in reading maps and globes. Pupils are also introduced to the geographic concepts of continent, country, state, and community.

BULLETIN-BOARD DISPLAY

Make a bulletin board entitled "We Live on the Earth." Collect pictures that show various physical features of the earth and the different people, plants, and animals that make their home on the earth.

In the center of the bulletin board, place a picture of a child or a group of children. Arrange the other pictures around this picture. Have labels ready to identify those pictures that illustrate vocabulary terms introduced in the chapter lessons.

GETTING STARTED

Call attention to the pictures on the bulletin-board display. Tell pupils that these pictures show some things about the earth. Discuss the different details that appear in each picture. Ask: *What does this picture tell you about the earth?*

LESSON 1 PAGES 2-5

GOALS
1. To know that the earth is made up of land and water. **2.** To understand that people, plants, and animals live on the earth. **3.** To understand that there are many different kinds of people on the earth.

READING VOCABULARY
earth, people, plants, animals

ORAL VOCABULARY
planet

TEACHING SUGGESTIONS
1. Vocabulary Development. Say to pupils, *Imagine you have just met a person from outer space and that person asked you where you lived. How would you answer that question?* As soon as the word *earth* is used, write it on the chalkboard. Develop the definition of *earth* as "the planet on which we live." Write the word *planet* on the chalkboard. Tell the pupils that they will be learning about the planet earth in this chapter.

2. Reading. Have pupils take turns reading the sentences on p. 2 aloud. Ask the following questions and have pupils read the sentence that answers each question.
a. *Where do we live?*
b. *What is the earth?*
c. *What do the pictures show?*
d. *Who lives on the earth?*
e. *What is the earth made of?*

3. Picture Reading. Have pupils look at the pictures on pp. 4–5 and tell what they see. List on the chalkboard all the living things pupils identify. Discuss the fact that along with many different people, there are many different kinds of plants and animals living on the earth. Have pupils read the sentences on the pages.

4. Art. Have pupils draw a picture of the earth to send to someone who lives on another planet. The picture should show what the earth is made of and some of the things that live on the earth. Arrange to display the pictures in the classroom.

LESSON 2 PAGES 6-11

GOALS
1. To understand that the earth has different physical features. **2.** To identify in a drawing an example of each of the following: plain, hill, mountain, ocean, lake, river, island, and peninsula. **3.** To compare and contrast some of the physical features of the earth.

READING VOCABULARY
plain, hill, mountain, ocean, river, lake, island, peninsula

ORAL VOCABULARY
landform, steep, area

TEACHING SUGGESTIONS
1. Picture Reading. Introduce this lesson by telling pupils that the earth is made of areas of land and bodies of water. Tell pupils that they will learn about three major landforms. Have them look at the picture on p. 6 and describe the kind of land shown. Write the descriptions on the chalkboard. Then write the word *plains* above the description. Have pupils read the sentences on p. 6 and discuss reasons why this land is good for farming.

Introduce the words *hills* and *mountains* by writing each on the chalkboard. Have pupils look at the pictures on p. 7 and describe what they see in each picture. List the descriptions of the hills and of the mountains under the correct word. Ask:
a. *In what ways do hills and mountains look alike?*
b. *In what ways do they look different?*
You may want to introduce the word *steep* at this point in the discussion.

2. Discussion. Ask the following questions:

a. *Do you think there are many farms in the mountains?*

b. *What kinds of work and activities might people do who live on a mountain? Would people who live on the plains do those same things?* Bring out the idea that people who live in different places on the earth may also do different things.

• **3. Writing.** Ask pupils to write a few sentences telling in which of these three areas they would most like to live. Have them explain why they want to live in that particular place. Allow pupils to share their ideas with the rest of the class. For pupils who have difficulty with creative writing, you may wish to have them find pictures of the area in which they would most like to live.

4. Picture Reading. Introduce the word *ocean*. Direct attention to the picture on p. 8. Ask: *Can you tell from this picture some of the things people near the ocean like to do?* After allowing time for silent reading, have pupils take turns reading the text on p. 8 aloud.

Continue with oral reading on p. 9. Ask pupils why one body of water is called a lake and another body of water is called a river. Define the words *lake* and *river*. Ask pupils to name the river pictured on p. 9.

5. Discussion. Lead a discussion focusing on the recreational aspects of oceans, lakes, and rivers. Encourage pupils to talk about pictures and relate their personal experiences. Ask: *What are some of the ways in which bodies of water are used for fun?*

6. Reading. Select several pupils to read aloud the first three sentences on p. 10. Emphasize the definition of *island*.

Introduce the term *peninsula*. Call on volunteers to read aloud the remaining sentences on p. 10.

7. Discussion. Have pupils look at the pictures on p. 10. Ask:

a. *How are these pictures alike?*

b. *How are they different?*

c. *Why do you think people would choose to live near water?*

8. Vocabulary Development. Write the following list of vocabulary words on a set of cards: *plain, ocean, island, mountain, hill, lake, river, peninsula.* Write the definitions for the words on a separate set of cards. Select two teams of eight children. Give one team the set of vocabulary word cards and the other team the set of definition cards. Have a child from the vocabulary team show his or her card; have the other team show the definition card that matches the vocabulary word. For variety, reverse the procedure and have pupils show a definition card first.

9. Map Reading. Have pupils read aloud the sentences on p. 11. Then select pupils to choose one word listed on the page, pronounce the word, and locate the physical feature on the picture map.

10. Group Work. Have pupils make a picture dictionary illustrating the eight vocabulary terms. Arrange the pictures on a chart or bulletin board under the proper vocabulary word. After each word, print a definition. Allow pupils to choose the word they want to illustrate, making sure that there is at least one picture for every defined word.

LESSON 3 PAGES 12–13

GOALS

1. To compare information shown in a photograph with information shown on a map. **2.** To know the difference between a map and a photograph. **3.** To understand that map symbols stand for real things and places. **4.** To use a map key to determine the meaning of map symbols. **5.** To draw and key a simple map.

READING VOCABULARY

map, symbol, key

TEACHING SUGGESTIONS

1. Discussion. Ask pupils to pretend they have just moved to a new town or city. Have them name different ways to find out about the community. List suggestions on the chalkboard. Guide discussion to include the following:

a. *What do the people do for a living?*
b. *What do the people do for fun?*
c. *What is the school like?*
d. *What are the stores like?*

2. Reading. Have pupils read the text on pp. 12–13. Develop the concepts of map, symbol, and key. Have pupils name each symbol in the key, find it on the map, and then find something each symbol stands for in the picture.

3. Discussion. Have pupils look at the picture on p. 12 and tell how it is like the map on p. 13. Then have them tell how it is different. Ask:

a. *Can you learn more about an area from a map or from a picture?*
b. *Can you learn more by using the map and the picture together than by using either one alone?*

4. Making a Map. Have pupils make simple maps of their school grounds. Have them indicate the playground area with a color and show that color as a symbol on the key. Have them indicate other structures with other colors.

LESSON 4   PAGES 14–15

GOALS

1. To understand that the earth is a sphere. **2.** To know that a globe is a model of the earth. **3.** To identify land and water areas on a globe.

READING VOCABULARY
space, globe, model

ORAL VOCABULARY
sphere

TEACHING SUGGESTIONS

1. Picture Reading. Have the pupils look at the picture on p. 14. Then ask:
a. *What does this picture show?*
b. *Where do you think this picture was taken? How can you tell?*

2. Reading/Vocabulary Development. Direct pupils to the sentences on p. 14. Have them read the first two sentences aloud. Write the word *space* and its definition on the chalkboard. Continue the activity by having pupils read aloud the last two sentences on p. 14. Discuss the earth's shape and introduce the word *sphere*. Ask children to find an item in the classroom that has the shape of a sphere (globe).

3. Group Work. Display a variety of models such as trucks, cars, airplanes, or doll-house furniture. Have pupils examine the models and discuss the similarities and differences between the models and the objects represented by the models. Lead the pupils in a discussion that will help them reach the following conclusions:

a. *A model has the same shape as the object it represents.*
b. *A model is usually much smaller than the object it represents.*

4. Reading. Have pupils look at the picture of the primary globe on p. 15. Ask them to read silently the first two sentences on p. 15 and find the meaning of the word *globe*. Ask: *What does the globe show?* Have pupils read the remaining sentences.

● **5. Research.** Have available picture books and storybooks about maps and globes. For those who require a challenge, you may wish to have them read and report on using maps and globes.

LESSON 5   PAGES 16–19

GOALS

1. To locate the North and South Poles on a map or globe. **2.** To understand the directions north and south. **3.** To understand the directions east and west. **4.** To explain what an explorer is. **5.** To use directions to identify parts of a map. **6.** To give examples of two pairs of opposites.

READING VOCABULARY
North Pole, northern, north, direction, South Pole, southern, south, opposite, explorer

ORAL VOCABULARY
polar region

TEACHING SUGGESTIONS
1. Demonstration. Display a globe in the classroom. Ask the pupils to turn to p. 16 in their book and locate the picture of a globe. Give the following explanation:
a. *People use a globe to find different places on the earth.*
b. *The children in the picture are finding two special places on the globe.*
c. *In this lesson, they will learn about these two special places.*
2. Reading Comprehension/Vocabulary Development. Before pupils read p. 16 silently and then aloud, introduce the word *direction*. After p. 16 has been read aloud, tell pupils that these poles are not things that one can touch or see, such as telephone poles. Explain that the poles are invisible except on globes and maps.

Ask pupils to explain what *north* is. Pupils' responses should include the facts that north is a direction and that movement toward the North Pole is north. Check pupils' understanding of the North Pole by asking, *Can you touch the North Pole?*

Introduce p. 17 by writing the word *opposite* on the chalkboard and by having the pupils help formulate a definition. Write the word on the chalkboard. Ask different pupils to give an example of two things that are opposite. After the page has been read aloud, check comprehension and un-

derstanding of vocabulary words by asking the following questions:
a. *What is south?*
b. *Where is the South Pole on the globe?*
c. *Does the direction north have an opposite?*
d. *What is the opposite of the South Pole? Of the North Pole?*

3. Using a Globe. Point out the location of the North Pole on the globe. Have pupils come to the globe and put their finger on the location of the North Pole and that of the South Pole. Point to the location of your state on the globe. Then have pupils put their finger on this location. Relate this location to the North Pole. Ask: *Which way is north?* Use the globe to develop the answer. *Which way is south?* Identify the north and south walls of the classroom and label them with signs.

4. Vocabulary Development. This activity will provide experience in using directions that are related to the individual pupil. Select a Treasure Hunter from the class. Have the Hunter close his or her eyes. Hide a "Treasure" somewhere in the room. Then direct the Hunter "with eyes open" toward the hidden treasure. Use only the following directions: *forward, backward, left, right, opposite.* When the Treasure has been found, select a new Hunter and repeat the activity. Use the activity to give practice with left and right and to extend or reinforce the concept of opposite.

5. Vocabulary Development. To include *up* and *down* in the experience of the pupils, use the game Guide the Pilot. Select one pupil to be the pilot and another to be the guide. The guide uses the directions forward (or front), backward (or back), left, right, up, down. For up, the pilot can be guided to step over a pile of books or some other small obstacle. For down, he or she can crawl under a table or desk or under an arch or tunnel formed by other pupils facing each other and joining hands.

6. Vocabulary Development. Write the word *explorer* on the chalkboard. Ask pupils to find the word in their book glossary or a classroom dictionary. Discuss the definition. *What does an explorer do?* The pupils' responses should include the idea that an explorer is one who goes in search of a place, a thing, or information.

7. Writing. Ask the pupils to write a story about living or visiting a polar region. Share the completed writings with the class by reading some stories orally and by mounting others for display.

8. Story Hour. Read the book *First to the Top of the World: Admiral Peary at the North Pole* by Tom Lisker. This reading can be extended to seven sessions by reading one chapter a day.

LESSON 6   PAGES 20–21

GOALS
1. To understand the relationship between east, west, south, and north. **2.** To identify east and west on a picture of a globe.

READING VOCABULARY
east, west

ORAL VOCABULARY
compass

TEACHING SUGGESTIONS
1. Reading Comprehension. Write the words *directions*, *east*, and *west* on the chalkboard. Tell the class, *Today we will learn about two more directions that are named east and west.* Tell the pupils to read the sentences on p. 20 silently. Then have pupils take turns showing the directions east and west on the globe. Ask: *What other directions are shown on the globe? Which directions are opposite each other?*

Have the pupils read the first sentence on p. 21 to find out how the sun helps us find east and west. Use the directional signs in the drawing on p. 21 to help pupils understand east and west. Ask pupils to point to the north arrow in the drawing. Then tell children to look at the right side of the drawing. Ask: *In which direction are you now looking? Look to the left and find the direction named.*

2. Vocabulary Development. Write the words for the four cardinal directions (north, south, east, and west) on the chalkboard. Label the classroom walls with each of the cardinal directions. Tell the pupils to face the north wall. Remind pupils that when facing north, east is to the right, west is to the left, and south is behind them. Have the pupils play a version of the game Simon Says, using the four cardinal directions. For example: "Simon says turn and face the south." "Simon says point toward the east." "Simon says take two steps toward the south."

3. Following Directions. Give each pupil a sheet of paper labeled with the cardinal directions. Have pupils follow oral directions as given. Examples:

a. *Put your name in the northern part of the paper.*

b. *Draw a circle in the southern part of the paper.*

c. *Draw a square on the eastern part of the paper.*

d. *Draw a large X on the western part of the paper.*

After all directions have been given, show pupils a copy of how their completed paper should look and let them check their answers.

4. Filmstrip. You may wish to use "Using Globes—Learning About East and West" (set 1 of *Map and Globe*, McGraw-Hill Films). In this film a toy duck helps teach directions; the word *we* is used as a memory cue for *west* and *east*.

5. Story Hour. Have children read *North, South, East, and West* by Franklyn M. Branley.

GOALS

1. To name and locate the earth's seven continents on a map. **2.** To name and locate the Atlantic, Pacific, Arctic, and Indian oceans on a map or globe. **3.** To understand the ways in which maps and globes are alike and are different. **4.** To understand that small areas on a map represent large areas on the earth.

READING VOCABULARY

divided, continent

ORAL VOCABULARY

world

TEACHING SUGGESTIONS

1. Map Reading. Have pupils look at the map on pp. 22–23. Ask:

a. *What does the map show?*

b. *What do the colors on the map represent?* Review the use of color as a symbol.

2. Vocabulary Development. Write the words *divided* and *continent* on the chalkboard and have pupils learn their pronunciation. Then display an apple (or draw one on the board) and ask, *What happens to the apple if it is divided?* Compare the apple to the land on earth and develop the understanding that the land on earth is divided into separate parts called continents.

3. Reading. Select pupils to read aloud the paragraph on p. 22. Then ask a pupil to use the map to locate each continent by name. Write the names on the chalkboard. Repeat the procedure with p. 23.

4. Discussion. Discuss the differences between the words *earth* and *world. Earth* is a physical or geographical term for the planet; *world* suggests the social and human aspects of the earth.

5. Using a Globe. Have a primary globe available in the classroom. Working with a few children at a time, have them examine the globe and locate each continent and ocean. Then ask, *How are the globe and the map in your textbook alike? How are they different?*

6. Using a Map and Globe. Arrange to display a simple map of the earth like the one shown in the text. Choose a place on the map and put a colored pin at that place. Tell the children to pretend that they will be flying around the world. Ask: *In which direction will you fly? Which continents and oceans will you fly over?* Vary the activity by starting the children at different places and having them travel in different directions.

Repeat this activity using a primary globe. Ask the children to tell why the globe gives them more of a feeling that they are really traveling around the earth. Also ask them if they think the continents and oceans are the same size as they appear to be on a globe. Remind pupils that the globe is only a very small model of the earth; this means that small areas and short distances on a globe are actually large areas and great distances on the earth.

7. Making a Mobile. To help pupils learn to recognize the shapes of the continents, have them make a mobile. Using a globe and the map in the textbook, help pupils to draw the shape of each continent on a separate piece of poster board. Have children color each continent a different color, label each continent with the correct name, and cut them out. Have pupils attach a string to each shape and tie the strings to a coat hanger. Display the mobiles.

8. Map Game. Play a game to help children learn the names of the continents and oceans and their location on the globe. Write the names of the continents and oceans on separate pieces of paper. Put all the pieces of paper in a box. Have pupils take turns choosing one piece of paper and locating the continent or ocean on the classroom globe.

LESSON 8 PAGES 24–25

GOALS

1. To name the continent on which the United States is located. **2.** To name and locate on a map Canada and Mexico. **3.** To understand the symbolism of a national flag.

READING VOCABULARY

country, United States, Mexico, Canada, neighbor, flag

ORAL VOCABULARY

nation

TEACHING SUGGESTIONS

1. Vocabulary Development. Discuss with pupils the meaning of *nation*. Write on the chalkboard the definition agreed on by the class. Then write the word *country* on the chalkboard. Ask, *What country do we live in?* Point out that *country* and *nation* are often used interchangeably.

2. Map. Have pupils look at the map on p. 24.

a. *What does the map show?*

b. *How are colors used on the map?*

c. *What colors are used to show the United States, Canada, and Mexico?*

3. Using a Globe. Review the concept of *continent* by having children locate the seven continents on a globe. Call attention to the two continents that have America in their name. Ask: *Why is one continent called North America and the other called South America?*

4. Reading. Have pupils read the first two paragraphs on p. 25 and point to each country on the map as it is mentioned. Ask the following questions:

a. *In what country do we live?*

b. *What country is south of the United States?*

c. *What country is north of the United States?*

d. *What countries are our neighbors?*

5. Discussion. Talk about the idea that just as people have neighbors who live near them, so do countries. Ask pupils to name some ways in which our country can be a good neighbor to Canada and to Mexico. Write their answers on the chalkboard in the form of a short paragraph.

6. Writing. Begin by telling the children that when we write or speak, we arrange our words in sentences. Sentences help others understand what we mean.

Write the following groups of words on the chalkboard. Have pupils write the words in correct sentence order, adding correct end punctuation.

a. We the United States in live (*We live in the United States.*)

b. is North America in Mexico (*Mexico is in North America.*)

c. neighbor northern is our Canada (*Canada is our northern neighbor./Our northern neighbor is Canada.*)

7. Reading. Have pupils read the last paragraph on p. 25. Point to the flag of Canada (left), the United States (middle), and Mexico (right). *What does each country have? Why is a flag called a symbol?*

8. Art. Have pupils make American flags using crayons, paint, or construction paper. Display their flags in the classroom.

● **9. Discussion.** Have pupils turn back to p. 1 and study the picture as you read the poem. Ask: *What is the poem about?* Encourage pupils to express their ideas about the meaning of the poem.

For those pupils who require a challenge, you may wish to have them learn one verse of the poem and recite it to the class.

LESSON 9 PAGES 26–29

GOALS

1. To know that the United States is divided into fifty parts called states. **2.** To locate the pupils' state on a map of the

United States. **3.** To develop respect for our nation—past and present. **4.** To sing, as a group, a song about our country.

READING VOCABULARY
state, Americans

ORAL VOCABULARY
history

TEACHING SUGGESTIONS
1. Reading. Ask pupils to read the sentences on pp. 26–27. Then ask them the following questions.
a. *What does the map show?*
b. *How can you tell that it is a map of the United States?* (Be sure someone mentions that the map has a title.)
c. *How many states does our country have?*
d. *What is the name of the state we live in? Who can find our state on the map?*
2. Using a Map. Tell the pupils that you want them to use their map to name the fifty states. As pupils name the states, write them on the chalkboard. Have pupils check the list on the chalkboard and their map to identify the states that have not been named. Continue until all fifty states have been named.

Make sure the children realize that Alaska and Hawaii are states of the United States. Have pupils find these states on a globe so they will see their location in relation to the other states. Explain why insets are used to show these states on some maps.
3. Discussion. Ask pupils to bring to class a list of states that they have visited. Initiate a discussion about why these particular places were visited.
4. Making a Chart. Use poster board to make a chart showing the states that have been visited by the pupils.
5. Reading. Have pupils read aloud the paragraphs on p. 28. Ask, *What is another name for our country? What are people called who live in the United States?* Be sure children understand that they are all Americans.
6. Picture Reading. Have children look at the picture on p. 28 and describe what they see. Help pupils understand the significance of visiting the Washington Monument. Introduce the concept of our history and develop its definition as the story of a nation. Bring out the idea that people honor our nation by visiting historical places; you might mention Washington, D.C., or a place of special interest in your own area. People also honor our nation by celebrating special holidays that are a part of our history (Fourth of July, Thanksgiving, Columbus Day).
7. Music. In addition to teaching the children to sing "This Land Is Your Land," you may want to have them learn a patriotic song such as "America, the Beautiful," "America," or "The Star-Spangled Banner."

LESSON 10 PAGES 30–33

GOALS
1. To locate Florida on a map of the United States. **2.** To use symbols and labels to identify five features (attractions) in Florida. **3.** To know the nickname, state bird, and state flower for Florida and for the pupils' state. **4.** To know that a state is made up of large and small communities.

READING VOCABULARY
Florida, nickname, community

ORAL VOCABULARY
mockingbird, orange blossom

TEACHING SUGGESTIONS
1. Using a Map. Have pupils locate

Florida on the map of the United States on pp. 26–27. Help them to recognize that Florida is one of the most southern states in the nation. Ask them to tell what is north, south, east, and west of the state. Ask, *Is Florida a peninsula?* Have pupils explain their answers.

While children are looking at the United States map, have them find their own state and describe its directional relationship to Florida. You may want to introduce the directions north *and* west as *northwest* and the directions north *and* east as *northeast*.

2. Reading. Have pupils read the sentences on p. 30 and ask:

a. *What does this map show?*

b. *What is Florida?*

c. *What will the map key tell us about Florida?*

3. Using a Map. Have pupils study the map key and name the places that people come to see in Florida. Then have them locate each place on the map.

● **4. Speaking.** Give the children who have visited Florida an opportunity to tell their classmates about their trip. Encourage them to bring in any brochures or postcards that they may have collected on their trip.

Ask other pupils to tell about places they have visited, perhaps focusing on the parks, historical buildings, or places of scenic interest that are located in their state. Bring out the understanding that each state has places of special interest to people.

You may wish to have pupils who require a challenge write a story about the place in Florida they would most like to visit. You may want to start them with the sentence idea, "I want to visit _____ because. . . ."

5. Reading. Ask pupils to take turns reading aloud the sentences on p. 32. Then discuss the following questions with them.

a. *Does each state have a nickname?* (Be sure pupils understand that each state does not have the same nickname.)

b. *What else does each state have besides a nickname?*

c. *What is Florida's state bird? What is Florida's state flower?* (Refer pupils to the pictures on the page.)

6. Reading. Have pupils read the sentences on p. 33 and then answer the following questions.

a. *What does each state have?* If necessary, explain the difference between city and town emphasizing primarily the idea of size.

b. *What is a community?* Tell pupils that they will be learning much more about communities in their social studies class this year.

c. *What is the name of our community?*

7. Using a Map. Have pupils turn to the map of Florida on p. 30 and find the symbol for cities in the map key. *How many cities are shown on the map?* Ask children to name the cities, then list the names on the chalkboard.

Using the map, review cardinal directions by asking questions such as,

a. *Which two cities are north of Orlando?*

b. *Which city is the most southern?*

c. *Is St. Petersburg on the east coast or the west coast of Florida?*

8. Using a Map. Display a large map of your state. Help pupils find their community on the map and mark the location with a colored pin. Also locate and mark neighboring communities that the children know. *In which direction would you travel from your community to _____?* Discuss reasons why people might travel to those other communities.

9. Letter Writing. In preparation for the study of communities in the next chapter, help the pupils write a letter to the town or city hall or to the local chamber of commerce requesting a map of your community.

Living in Communities

CHAPTER 2

LIVING IN COMMUNITIES

Dear Parent,

Your child is starting a new chapter in *Neighborhoods and Communities* called "Living in Communities." This chapter looks at the community as a place where people live and work together. The topics in this chapter include the kinds of communities, such as cities, towns, suburbs, and farms; the types of houses people live in; and the kinds of buildings and facilities families in a community depend on. Your child will also explore places, such as parks, museums, and zoos, where people can learn and have fun.

To help your child discover things about your community, take your child on a guided tour. Point out libraries, hospitals, fire departments, and different kinds of stores. If you live in a farming community, tell how your needs for these facilities are met. Talk about some things you and your neighbors do to help the community. Take a picture of a special place or building for your child to show in class. This interest and involvement on your part can add greatly to your child's understanding of your community.

Sincerely,

CHAPTER 2 PAGES 38–71

LIVING IN COMMUNITIES

THEME

In all parts of the world people live in groups called communities.

OVERVIEW

People live in communities to be near other people. They share community facilities and live and work together. Communities help people meet their basic needs. In this chapter the concept of community is defined in terms of families, neighbors, neighborhoods, workers, houses, schools, and other buildings. Different kinds of communities, such as cities, suburbs, towns, and farming areas, are studied.

BULLETIN-BOARD DISPLAY

Prepare a mural background of a long road with houses and trees along it or make a city street scene with apartment houses. Label the mural *About Our Neighborhood, Where We Live,* or *We Live in a Community.*

Have pupils work in pairs and trace around each other's shoe on construction paper. Then have them cut out their shoe print and write their name and address on it. Tape the shoe prints on the path or street in the mural.

GETTING STARTED

Read the poem on p. 38. Ask pupils to study the picture on pp. 38–39 and tell what they see. Start a discussion by asking pupils to describe what a community is. Tell pupils that the picture shows a community in New York City. The people are having a street festival. Help pupils conclude that a community is a group of people living near and interacting with one another.

GOALS

1. To define *community.* **2.** To compare their own community to those pictures. **3.** To describe how communities are alike and different. **4.** To arrange a list of community features in alphabetical order.

READING VOCABULARY
community

ORAL VOCABULARY
urban, suburban, fishing village, rural

TEACHING SUGGESTIONS

1. Reading/Discussion. Have pupils turn to p. 40 and read the text. Use the annotation on p. 40 to bring out the point that communities are alike and different. Explain that the size of a community is usually determined by the amount of land and the number of people. Ask: *Which community on these pages is largest? In which of the communities might there be the most people?*

2. Vocabulary Development. On the chalkboard write the words *urban, suburban, fishing village,* and *rural.* Have pupils study the picture on p. 40. Tell pupils that this is an urban community. Families in this community live near other families.

Focus attention on the picture at the top of the next page. Explain that it is a suburban community. Ask: *How is a suburban community different from an urban community?*

Continue this questioning procedure for the fishing village and the rural community. Ask: *How are the communities on pp. 40–41 like each other? How are they different? Which community is most like yours?*

3. Vocabulary Development. With the help of the class make a list of community features shown in each picture. Have pupils tell exactly what they see. List such things as land, houses, and stores. Have pupils copy the list and arrange the features in alphabetical order.

● **4. Poetry.** Have pupils turn back to pp. 38–39. Have them study the picture as you read the poem aloud. Call on pupils to read the lines of the poem that ask a question.

For pupils who need a challenge, ask them to write a poem about their own neighborhood or community and read it to the class.

For pupils who have difficulty, you may wish to have them draw a picture of one thing they would like to have a visitor know about their community.

GOALS

1. To understand that people who live near each other are neighbors. **2.** To define *neighborhood.* **3.** To list ways in which people in a neighborhood help one another. **4.** To identify neighborhood as a part of a large community.

READING VOCABULARY
neighbor, neighborhood

ORAL VOCABULARY
recreation, interest

TEACHING SUGGESTIONS

1. Vocabulary Development. Write the words *neighbor* and *neighborhood* on the chalkboard. Tell pupils that one way of looking at a neighborhood is to think of it as the area within walking distance of their home. (This concept applies more to cities and towns than to rural areas.) Ask them to name places in their area that are within walking distance—for example, parks, schools, houses, and stores. List the places on the chalkboard. Explain that people who live within walking distance of one another are *neighbors* and that the area within walking distance is their *neighborhood*. Help pupils understand that their neighborhood is one of several that make up a larger community.

2. Picture Reading. Call attention to the picture at the top of p. 42. Ask:

a. *Do you think these people are neighbors? How can you tell?*

b. *When do people in your neighborhood get together?*

c. *What do they do on these occasions?* Have pupils draw a picture of something they do with their neighbors.

3. Community Resources. Read the text on p. 43. Ask pupils to name things families in their community do together for recreation. Write the responses on the chalkboard. Ask: *What are the people in this picture doing?*

4. Filmstrip. Show the filmstrip *Taking a Walk in the Community*, in which the activities of a typical community are explored.

5. Art. Have pupils make a drawing of something families in a community do together. Display the drawings on the wall or bulletin board.

6. Oral Reporting. Have pupils tell the class about their own neighborhood. They should begin with their home address and then describe the kinds of buildings in the area and what they like most about their neighborhood.

7. Writing. Tell pupils to study the picture at the bottom of pp. 42–43. Explain that neighbors work together to make their neighborhood a better place to live. Ask pupils what they can do to improve things for their family or neighborhood. Tell them to copy the following "contract" from the chalkboard and fill in the blanks. *I, (name), agree to help my family, friends, and community. The family member I will help is _____ . For this person I will _____ . One thing I will do for my community is _____ .*

LESSON 3 PAGES 44–45

GOALS
1. To understand that communities have several types of houses. **2.** To compare and contrast different kinds of shelter in which people live. **3.** To understand that shelter is a basic need of all people. **4.** To distinguish houses from other types of buildings. **5.** To arrange sentences in proper sequence.

READING VOCABULARY
apartment building, houseboat, house trailer

ORAL VOCABULARY
shelter

TEACHING SUGGESTIONS
1. Vocabulary Development. Take pupils for a walk around the neighborhood. Point out different kinds of buildings. Help pupils distinguish houses from other kinds of buildings. After returning to the classroom, discuss some of the houses seen. Have pupils describe houses they have seen in other neighborhoods, in other parts of the country, or in books. Write the words *house, shelter,* and *home* on the chalkboard. Ask: *What is a house? A shelter? A home?* (Accept all reasonable answers.) Help pupils conclude that communities have many places for people to live.

2. Group Work. Help pupils construct a playhouse from building blocks or a cardboard box. Make a floor plan for the house. Include dining room, bedrooms, kitchen, bathroom, and so on. Help pupils create a make-believe family to live in the playhouse. Name the family members and describe their relationship to each other.

3. Making a Map Key. Tell each pupil to make a map key for the playhouse by drawing symbols to stand for each room. For example, a stove or sink could stand for the kitchen and a bed or dresser for the bedroom.

4. Art. Have pupils draw pictures of their homes on poster board. Help them label their drawings with name, address, and telephone number. Display the drawings on the walls or bind them in a "class directory."

5. Sentence Sequence. Write simple sentences from the lesson on index cards, one sentence per card. Example: *Some people live in trailer homes.* Shuffle the cards and clip them together. Make them available for individual children to put in sentence order.

6. Research. Have pupils collect pictures from magazines or newspapers that show houses from different environments. These pictures may be made into a huge collage with the title *Homes.* Animal homes might be included to add enjoyment.

7. Story Hour. Read *The True Book of Houses* by Katherine Carter. This book is about houses in hot lands and cold lands, farm and city houses, and houses of long ago.

LESSON 4   PAGES 46–49

GOALS

1. To use a dictionary to find the meaning of a word. **2.** To identify ways in which pupils get to school. **3.** To understand the purpose of school. **4.** To name skills pupils learn at school. **5.** To tell how these skills will help them. **6.** To make a simple graph.

READING VOCABULARY
school, learning, citizen

ORAL VOCABULARY
education

TEACHING SUGGESTIONS
1. Vocabulary Development. Introduce this lesson by asking a question such as: *Why do children go to school?* Lead pupils in a discussion about why they go to school and what they learn. (To learn to read, write, count, and get along with others) Write the word *education* on the chalkboard. Help pupils find the word in the dictionary and discuss its meaning with them.

2. Picture Reading. Have children study the pictures on p. 46–47. Ask: *What are the children in these pictures doing? Which school probably serves a larger community? Why do you think so?* Look at the picture at the bottom of p. 47. Ask: *What does this picture show about how children get to school?* Have pupils compare the ways they get to school with those pictured. Ask: *How many of you walk to school? Ride a bus? Ride a bicycle? Ride with parents?*

● **3. Making a Graph.** On the chalkboard, list the ways pupils in your class get to school and the number that travel each way.

For those pupils who require a challenge, you may wish to have them make a bar graph from the above information.

4. Oral Expression. Ask pupils who have attended another school to tell how it was similar or different from the school they now attend. Lead children to conclude that in most communities in our country there are schools and that most boys and girls today go to school.

5. Discussion. Direct attention to pp. 48–49. Ask the following questions.
a. *What do these pictures show?*
b. *What do you think the children are learning?*
c. *Who is their helper?*

● **6. Art.** Distribute sheets of cardboard or oaktag, crayons, scissors, and manila envelopes. Have the pupils draw a picture of how they learn in class. Suggest that they choose one activity to portray in their drawing. Cut the picture into pieces to make a jigsaw puzzle and place each puzzle in a manila envelope. The pupil's name should be written on the flap of the envelope. The puzzles can be placed in the Game Center along with sheets of writing paper and pencils. Have pupils take one envelope at a time and put the puzzle together. For those who require a challenge, you may wish to have them write a poem or story about the subject of the puzzle.

7. Writing. Write the address of the school on the chalkboard. Call attention to the words that are written with capital letters. Help the pupils make a record of places that are familiar to them by completing the following sentences.

a. *The name of my school is. . . .*
b. *The community I live in is. . . .*
c. *I live in the state of. . . .*

8. Making a Map. Have pupils make a map of their school. Label each room and display the map on a bulletin board. Using a length of yarn and pushpins, pupils can take turns indicating routes from room to room. Have them follow directions such as the following: *Show a route from the second-grade classroom to the cafeteria.*

Also give pupils directions for a particular route. For example:

a. *Show how you would turn left from our classroom to find the first-grade classroom.*
b. *Show the route from this room to the principal's office.*

If cardinal directions are included on the map, ask questions such as: *If you were in the library, in which direction would you go to get to the gymnasium?*

LESSON 5   PAGES 50–51

GOALS
1. To define the word *goods*. **2.** To name goods purchased by families. **3.** To name the kinds of goods that can be purchased in stores in the community. **4.** To identify pictorial material.

READING VOCABULARY
goods

ORAL VOCABULARY
shopping center, window shopping

TEACHING SUGGESTIONS
1. Discussion. Begin the discussion by asking pupils to name the different kinds of stores found in their community. Make a list of the stores on the chalkboard—for example, bakery, grocery, supermarket, card store. Explain that these stores sell goods and that goods are things people buy that they need or want.

2. Picture Reading. Have pupils look at the first picture on p. 50 and tell what they see. Ask: *What kinds of stores sell food?* Point to the bottom picture. Ask: *What are the people in this picture doing? Do you know what window shopping means?* Explain that window shopping is looking at goods from the outside of the store. Ask: *What goods can these people see in the window? Have you ever spent time window shopping?* Direct pupils' attention to the picture on p. 51. Ask pupils to tell what they see. Ask: *Are bicycles goods? Where would you go to buy a bicycle?*

3. Reading. Have pupils read p. 52 silently and name two kinds of goods that are sold in stores.

4. Discussion. Explain that in some small communities people cannot buy all the goods they need, so they must go to other communities to shop. Many people go to shopping centers. Some communities have shopping centers. Start a discussion by asking pupils the following:

a. *Is there a shopping center in your community?*
b. *Does your family shop at the shopping center?*
c. *What kinds of stores are in the shopping center?*

5. Field Trip. Take the class on a trip to a shopping center. After returning to the classroom, have pupils tell about some of the stores they saw.

6. Map Reading. Help pupils draw a map

of a shopping center. On a large sheet of construction paper, draw the shapes for the stores. Have pupils name the stores and label them, or have them cut out different shapes to represent the stores and paste the shapes to the map.

LESSON 6   PAGES 52–55

GOALS
1. To define *service*. 2. To discuss the importance of services to people in the community. 3. To identify some of the services that workers provide to people in the community. 4. To classify examples of goods and services. 5. To write photo captions.

READING VOCABULARY
service

ORAL VOCABULARY
fire fighter, mail carrier, police officer, nurse, sanitation worker, librarian

TEACHING SUGGESTIONS
1. Discussion. Review the meaning of *goods* with the class. Ask pupils if they know of things that families need or want done that others must do for them (collecting trash, delivering mail, and so on). Write their responses on the chalkboard. Tell pupils that things done for them by other people are called services.

2. Picture Reading. Have pupils look at the pictures on pp. 52–55 and name the services shown. Ask: *Which service helps sick people feel better?* Ask them to tell what other services are shown and to name the people who provide that service. Ask:
a. *Which worker deals with books and with learning?* (Librarian)
b. *Who is the worker who delivers the mail?* (Mail carrier)
c. *Who keeps the community clean and free of litter?* (Sanitation worker)

d. *Which worker would you call if your home were on fire?* (Fire fighter)

3. Writing. Ask the class to study the pictures and write one sentence about each service or service worker shown. To help pupils get started write the following sentences on the chalkboard.
a. *Mail carriers bring letters to people in our town.*
b. *The nurse helps when you are sick.*

4. Discussion. Ask:
a. *What do the workers in these pictures have in common?* (Each job involves doing something for other people.)
b. *Is each job important to others in the community? Why?*
c. *Do you think that you would like to do this kind of work?*

5. Career Awareness. Call on volunteers to role-play a service worker and let the class guess the service that is provided.

Read the following statements about the service workers in this lesson and have pupils indicate whether the statements are true or false.
a. *Mail carriers are important in our community because they print newspapers.*
b. *Librarians are important in our community because they help us find what we want in a department store.*
c. *Firefighters are important in our community because they deliver our mail.*

LESSON 7   PAGES 56–57

GOALS
1. To name places in a community where people go for recreation. 2. To define the word *museum*. 3. To find their state on a United States map. 4. To compare their community with another community.

READING VOCABULARY
museum

ORAL VOCABULARY
astronaut, spaceship

TEACHING SUGGESTIONS
1. Group Work. Divide the class into five groups. Have each group make a list of activities people can do in a park. Allow ample time; then have pupils report by group.

2. Reading. Tell pupils to read the first paragraph on p. 56 silently. Then call on a pupil to read the question aloud. Compare the list of activities that each group made with what is happening in the picture.

3. Story Hour. Read to the class *Around the World in 90 Minutes* by Rocco Feravolo. This story tells of two astronauts' journey in space.

4. Picture Reading. Direct pupils' attention to the space museum picture. Use the picture to introduce the word *museum*. Write museum on the chalkboard and have pupils talk about the kinds of museums they know about.

Tell pupils to look at the picture of the space museum again. Ask: *Why is it important to learn about outer space? Would you like to travel in a spaceship?*

5. Letter Writing. Help pupils compose and write a letter to the Alabama Space and Rocket Center, Tranquility Base, Huntsville, Alabama 35807. Pupils can request photographs and information on various trips into space.

6. Discussion. Ask pupils who have visited a zoo to tell about it. Ask: *What animals can you see at the zoo? Which animals could children have for pets?*

7. Role-Playing. Have small groups of pupils role-play zoo animals. Play background music as pupils assume the roles of animals and move to the music. Ask pupils who are observing to identify the animals. Let pupils take turns as animals and observers.

8. Reading. Call on a pupil to read the second sentence on p. 57. Call on other pupils

to name places in their community where people can have fun and learn. List the places on the chalkboard. Discuss the need for adequate maintenance of these places.

9. Art. Refer to the list of activities people do in the park. Divide the class into groups. Let each group choose a favorite park activity. Have pupils draw group pictures of the activity chosen.

10. Vocabulary Development. Have pupils name things that their community does not have, that they would like the community to have. Help them decide which things are possible and which are not.

11. Field Trip. Plan a trip to a zoo, park, or museum. Help pupils discover some things that the community has done to make the place a good one for learning and for recreation.

12. Filmstrip. Show the filmstrip *Fun in the City*. Pupils learn about various places where people can learn and also have fun.

LESSON 8   PAGES 58–59

GOALS
1. To describe some characteristics of a large city. **2.** To name some advantages and disadvantages of living in a large city. **3.** To find specific cities and states on a United States map.

READING VOCABULARY
city, typewriter, machine, factory

ORAL VOCABULARY
pollution, crowds, elevator

TEACHING SUGGESTIONS
1. Discussion. Write the words *city* and *urban* on the chalkboard. Tell pupils that some communities are large cities. Large cities are called urban communities. A large city is made up of small communities and neighborhoods.

2. Picture Reading. Have pupils look at the picture at the top of pp. 58–59. Tell them that it is a picture of New York City taken from an airplane. Ask:

a. *What kinds of buildings do you see?*
b. *How do people get to the top of these buildings?*
c. *What is the tallest building in the picture called?* (Empire State Building) Ask pupils who have visited this building to share their experience with the class.

3. Using a Map. Display a map of New York City and review the meaning of *island*.

Display a map of the United States and have pupils find New York State. Ask:

a. *In what part of the United States is the state of New York located?*
b. *In what state do we live?*
c. *In what direction is New York from our state?*

4. Reading. Have pupils read the text on the top of p. 58. Ask: *What are large communities called? What is the largest city in the United States?*

5. Discussion. Write the word *apartment* on the chalkboard. Ask:

a. *Why are these houses built close together?*
b. *What are they made of?*
c. *What jobs do you think the people that live here might have?*
d. *What do you think they might do for recreation?*
e. *What other types of homes are found in large cities?*

Discuss the reasons for wanting to live in a large city (jobs, recreation, shopping) and the reasons for not wanting to live in a large city (crowds, pollution, noise).

6. Picture Reading. Have pupils look at the pictures at the bottom of p. 59. Ask: *What do these pictures show?* After pupils describe the pictures, have them tell about the kinds of work the people do and ask if pupils would like to do that kind of work.

7. Reading. Have pupils read the paragraph at the bottom of p. 58. Ask: *Who uses this kind of machine in your school?*

8. Picture Reading. Tell pupils to look at the picture on p. 59. Explain that the factory is a part of a community. Ask: *What are the workers making? Why might a community have a factory?*

LESSON 9 PAGES 60–61

GOALS

1. To define *suburb*. **2.** To identify some characteristics of a suburban community. **3.** To name several means of transportation.

READING VOCABULARY
suburb, transportation

ORAL VOCABULARY
towns, traffic

TEACHING SUGGESTIONS

1. Using a Dictionary. Have pupils find the word *suburb* in the dictionary. Write the word and its meaning on the chalkboard. Explain that some cities and towns are located just outside a large city and that these cities and towns are called suburbs.

2. Reading. Have pupils read p. 60 to find out what the community is called and where it is located.

3. Picture Reading. After pupils have studied the picture, ask: *What kinds of buildings are these? How many families do you think live in each house?* Point to the next picture and ask: *What does this picture show? Where do you think these people might be going? What kinds of transportation are being used? What other ways can people get from the suburbs to nearby cities?*

4. Reading. Write the word *transportation* on the chalkboard. Ask pupils to name some kinds of transportation people use. Have the class read p. 61 to find out where people who live in the suburbs work.

5. Group Work. Help pupils build a model

of a suburban neighborhood. A large box or a table can serve as a base for the model. Pupils can make small cardboard cutouts to represent buildings.

6. Filmstrip. Show the filmstrip *Types of Cities: The Suburb.* Various features of a suburban community are shown in the filmstrip.

LESSON 10 PAGES 62–63

GOALS
1. To describe the characteristics of a rural community. **2.** To recognize rural communities as places with some similarities to other communities. **3.** To name food items grown on farms.

READING VOCABULARY
rural communities, town

ORAL VOCABULARY
pastureland, grazing

TEACHING SUGGESTIONS
1. Picture Reading. Have pupils study the pictures on pp. 62–63. Discuss the characteristics of rural areas and compare them with those of other communities studied.
2. Reading. Ask pupils to read p. 62 silently. Ask:
a. *How is land in farm communities used?*
b. *What happens to plants and animals that are raised on farms?*
c. *What does most of the food we eat come from?*
3. Vocabulary Development. Make two columns on the chalkboard and head them *Plants* and *Animals.* Call on pupils to name plants and animals that farmers raise for food. Also have them name other plants and animals that farmers raise for uses other than food.
4. Group Work. Divide the class into four teams. Assign each team a major food group (meats, fruits and vegetables, grains and cereals, and dairy products). Have

each group either find pictures in a magazine or draw and color pictures of foods that belong in their food group. Have the children paste the pictures on construction paper and display them on a bulletin board. The project may be called *Food Families* or *Rural Communities Provide Foods.*
5. Music. Teach the class to sing "The Barnyard" from *Silver Burdett Music 2,* 1981 ed., or "Old MacDonald Had a Farm."
6. Art. Help pupils make a mural of a rural community. Have some pupils design a small town and others depict the nearby farms.
7. Film. Show the film *The Farm Community* to the class. It shows how one farm family works and contributes to a rural community and what services the family receives in return.
8. Art. Have pupils make drawings of things farm families do for recreation. This can include picnicking, hiking, and fishing.

LESSON 11 PAGES 64–65

GOALS
1. To understand that a state is made up of many communities. **2.** To use symbols to identify cities on the map of Indiana. **3.** To name a state that borders Indiana.

READING VOCABULARY
Indiana

ORAL VOCABULARY
Michigan, Illinois, Ohio, Kentucky, shipping

TEACHING SUGGESTIONS
1. Reading a Map. Have pupils look at the map on page 65. Ask:
a. *What does this map show?*
b. *Is Indiana a state or a country?*
c. *Which is smaller, a state or a country?*

d. *Which states border Indiana?*

2. Thinking. Draw four concentric circles on the chalkboard. Starting with the outermost circle, number them from 1 to 4. Ask pupils which circle would represent their country, state, city, and town.

3. Reading. Have pupils read the sentence on p. 64 that tells which state is shown on the map; the sentence that tells what the map symbols show; and the sentences that ask a question.

Review with the class some characteristics of towns such as the following:

a. Towns are smaller than cities.

b. Towns have fewer jobs and recreational activities.

c. Towns offer clean air and open space.

d. Towns are less noisy and have fewer people.

4. Writing Skills. Ask pupils to copy on a sheet of paper the names of towns and cities from the map of Indiana. Have them arrange the names in alphabetical order.

LESSON 12   PAGES 66–67

GOALS

1. To recognize that the United States is made up of different groups of people.
2. To locate the continent of North America on the globe.

READING VOCABULARY
United States

ORAL VOCABULARY
background, language

TEACHING SUGGESTIONS

1. Discussion. Review the meaning of community with the class. Ask: *What makes a community? What would communities be like if there were no people?* Have pupils who are new to the community tell where they have come from and whether their former community is in the state in which they now live.

2. Using a Globe. Display the classroom globe. Have pupils find their continent. Name the other continents and help pupils find them on the globe. Ask pupils if any of their friends or neighbors have come from another country or continent. If so, find those places on the globe.

3. Speaking. Ask:

a. *How many communities have you lived in?*

b. *Have you lived in more than one place in this community?*

c. *Did you have to change schools?*

Explain that people came from all over the world to live in the United States and that they live in many different communities. Some people stay in one community, while other people move from one community to another.

4. Community Resources. Invite a person who has come to America from another country to visit the class. Have the person talk about his or her former community.

5. Picture Reading. Have pupils study the picture on p. 66 as you read the text aloud. Ask pupils to make some guesses about why people move from one community to another. Use the annotation on p. 66 to give pupils some indications about why people move.

Direct pupils' attention to the picture on p. 67. Stress the point that some large communities in the United States are made up of people from almost every country on earth.

6. Using a Map. Obtain a local map of the pupils' community. Have pupils locate their school and homes on the map. Use pushpins to indicate desired places. Display the map on a wall.

7. Making a Map. If a local community map is not available, pupils might enjoy working as a group to make one.

Working in Communities

CHAPTER 3

WORKING IN COMMUNITIES

Dear Parent,

All people have needs and wants. Food, clothes, and shelter are basic needs all people have. In our third chapter, called "Working in Communities," your child will be learning about how families satisfy their needs and wants. We will be learning about how money is used to buy what we need and want and about the many kinds of work people do to earn money. In addition, your child will learn how workers provide goods and services for themselves and others.

You might like to take your child on a shopping trip to a supermarket or clothing store. Explain why you choose one item over another. You might also like to discuss your job or the job of a family member.

This chapter will provide many opportunities for family discussions. I am sure your child will benefit greatly from these discussions.

Sincerely,

WORKING IN COMMUNITIES

THEME

People produce goods and services to earn an income. The income is used to buy needs and wants.

OVERVIEW

All people have wants and needs. They need goods and services. To get goods and services people do many different kinds of work.

In this chapter pupils are introduced to workers and the kinds of work people do. They will learn that by doing different kinds of work, more goods and services are available to all the people in a community.

BULLETIN-BOARD DISPLAY

Distribute magazines and have pupils find pictures of workers of various kinds—young and old, male and female. Include workers who make goods and those who provide services. Have a good mixture of jobs and workers that pupils are familiar with, as well as some unfamiliar ones. The unfamiliar occupations will serve as vocabulary builders and help pupils realize the many kinds of work people do. Display the pictures on the bulletin board.

GETTING STARTED

Set up a store in the classroom. Have pupils bring in old toys and books. Make certain the items are no longer wanted by the children. You might also have pupils make puppets and paint pictures. Help pupils make labels, put prices on the items, and display them on a table. Throughout this chapter give pupils an opportunity to work in the classroom store, as well as be customers.

GOALS
1. To define *needs*. 2. To define *wants*. 3. To distinguish between needs and wants. 4. To name three basic needs all people have. 5. To understand that all people do not need and want the same things.

READING VOCABULARY
needs, wants

ORAL VOCABULARY
survive, climate

TEACHING SUGGESTIONS
1. **Vocabulary Development.** Write the words *needs* and *wants* on the chalkboard. Ask pupils to tell what these words mean. Have pupils turn to the Glossary on pp. 180–181 and read the definition for each word.

2. **Reading.** Have pupils turn to p. 74 and read the text silently. Call on volunteers to read the sentences that tell what needs and wants are. Before having pupils answer the questions on p. 74, explain that all people do not need and want the same things. What one person considers a need may be a want to someone else.

3. **Picture Reading.** Read aloud the last paragraph on p. 74. Call on individual students to classify the pictures according to their own needs and wants.

• 4. **Research.** Distribute magazines and department-store catalogs and have pupils find pictures showing some of their own needs and wants. Have them paste the pictures on construction paper and present them to the class.

You may wish to have pupils who require a challenge write a short story about a want or need they may have.

5. **Picture Reading.** Direct pupils' attention to the picture on p. 76 and have them tell what they see. Explain that while most needs and wants differ, there are some needs that all people have. Ask the following questions:
a. *Do all people need food?*
b. *Why do people need food?*
c. *What would happen if people did not have food?* (They would die.)
d. *Do all people need the same kinds of foods?*

Direct pupils' attention to the pictures on p. 77, and ask questions similar to those you asked about food. Allow the class time to discuss the need for food, clothes, and shelter.

6. **Vocabulary Development.** Write the words *basic needs* and *survive* on the chalkboard. Tell pupils that *to survive* means "to live" or "to stay alive." Basic needs are the things people need to survive. Have pupils turn back to p. 76 and read the sentence that tells the three basic needs. On the chalkboard write *food, clothes,* and *shelter* under the heading "Basic Needs." Help pupils conclude that basic needs are those things all people must have to survive.

7. **Writing.** Write the following sentences on the chalkboard and have pupils copy the sentences and fill in the missing word.
a. All people need _____ to eat.
b. All people need _____ to wear.
c. All people need _____ to live in.

8. **Vocabulary Development.** This activity will help reinforce the idea that all people do not meet their basic needs the same way. Write the word *climate* on the chalkboard. Ask pupils if they know what climate means. Explain that *climate* means "the kind of weather a place has over a period of time." Stress that all climate is not the same. Some places are hot and dry; others are cold and wet. Climate helps determine the ways people meet their needs for food, clothes, and shelter.

9. **Research.** Distribute magazines to the class. Divide the class into three groups.

Assign *food* to one group, *clothes* to the second group, and *shelter* to the third group. Have pupils find pictures of how families in other parts of the world meet these basic needs. Call attention to differences in clothing and shelters used in hot, cold, wet, and dry places. Ask pupils for their ideas on why there are such differences. Stress that families from other parts of the world may eat different food, dress differently, and have different looking houses, but they still need food, clothes, and shelter to live.

Have each group present their pictures to the rest of the class. Each child in the group may point to the pictures he or she has found and tell something about them.

LESSON 2   PAGES 78–79

GOALS
1. To understand that needs vary from one person to another. **2.** To understand that people have emotional and personal needs. **3.** To describe one way families show love.

READING VOCABULARY
love, affection, friends

ORAL VOCABULARY
emotional, personal, kindness, companionship, protection

TEACHING SUGGESTIONS
1. Discussion/Picture Reading. Review basic needs with the class. Have pupils study the picture at the top of p. 78 while you read the text aloud. To help pupils understand that people have other needs, ask the following questions:
a. *What does the picture show?*
b. *How do you think the child feels?*
c. *How does the parent feel?*
d. *Do you sometimes need to be hugged?*
e. *Do you sometimes hug someone?*

Point out that hugging is a way of expressing love, affection, and kindness. Ask:
a. *What other ways do people show love for one another?* (By sharing, helping)
b. *In what ways do you help your family?* (Bring out the idea that children can help by taking care of a pet, helping with dishes, taking care of their toys and clothes.)
c. *In what ways does your family help you?* (By providing love, companionship, protection)
2. Art. Have pupils draw pictures showing how they show their love for a family member. Display the pictures on the bulletin board. Discuss parental and fraternal love with the class.
3. Picture Reading. Focus pupils' attention on the picture at the bottom of p. 78. Ask the following questions:
a. *Who do you look for when you want someone to play with?* (A friend)
b. *What things do friends do together?*
c. *Do you have fun with a friend?*
d. *Do you share things with a friend?*
e. *Does everyone need a friend?*
f. *Who else do you have fun with?* (Family, neighbors)
At this point you might want to review Chapter 2, Lesson 2, about things family members and neighbors do for recreation.
● **4. Creative Writing.** Have pupils bring in pictures from newspapers or magazines that show friends in everyday situations (playing together, at school, at home). Have pupils paste each picture on a separate sheet of paper and write a caption for each one.

You may wish to have pupils who require a challenge write a poem or a paragraph about one of their pictures.
5. Discussion/Picture Reading. Have pupils look at the picture on p. 79. Ask: *Do you think these children are friends? How can you tell?*

Use the annotation on p. 79 to help pupils understand that some people have needs that others do not have. Explain that people have personal needs. Ask: *What is different about the two children in the picture?* (One is wearing glasses.) Call on volunteers to name some other personal needs. Allow the class time to discuss some personal needs a friend or family member might have, such as a hearing aid, a wheelchair, or a guide dog.

6. Story Hour. Read *Love Is a Special Way of Feeling* by Joan Walsh Anglund.

LESSON 3   PAGES 80–81

GOALS
1. To understand that people work to earn money. **2.** To define *income*. **3.** To understand that money is used to buy needs and wants. **4.** To identify several different types of work people do.

READING VOCABULARY
income

ORAL VOCABULARY
career

TEACHING SUGGESTIONS
1. Vocabulary Development. Write the words *work* and *income* on the chalkboard. Ask pupils if they know what the word *work* means. Accept all reasonable answers. Encourage them to relate their personal experiences by talking about the different kinds of work adult family members do outside the home. Stress the fact that maintaining a home is also work.

Have pupils turn to the Glossary on pp. 182–183 and find the word *income*. Call on a pupil to read the definition to the class.
2. Discussion. Begin a discussion by asking the following:
a. *Why do people work?* (To earn money)
b. *Why do people need money?* (To buy what they need and want)

c. *What do people do to earn money?* (Work)
d. *What is the money that people earn called?* (Income)

Help pupils conclude that in our society money is what people use in exchange for the things they need and want.
3. Field Trip. Find out if any local industries allow visitors. If so, arrange to take pupils on a tour. If this is not convenient, take the class on a bus or walking tour around the community.

After returning to the classroom pose this question to the pupils: *How do people in our community make a living?* On the chalkboard list as many different ways as possible.
4. Picture Reading. Have pupils turn to pp. 80–81. Start with the first picture on p. 80 and ask the following questions:
a. *What does this picture show?*
b. *What kind of work is being done?*
c. *Do you know someone who does this kind of work?*
d. *Does everyone do this kind of work?*
e. *Do people do different kinds of work?*
f. *What kind of community is this kind of work done in?*

Continue this procedure for the other pictures on these two pages.
5. Music. Sing the following song with the class: "The Carpenter," *Silver Burdett Music 1*, 1981 ed., Record 8.
6. Discussion. Have pupils name some things their own family needs or wants to buy. Discuss where the money for these things comes from. Reinforce the ideas that money is used to buy what we need and want and that people work to earn money.
7. Career Awareness. This would be a good time to involve pupils in a career awareness discussion. Help them realize that by going to school they are preparing for work in the future. Let pupils choose the kind of work they think they would like to do when they grow up. Have them draw a picture of themselves doing the work.

Give pupils a chance to show their picture to the class and let the class try to guess what it is.

- **8. Poetry.** Have pupils turn back to p. 72 and read the poem silently. Call on volunteers to read the poem aloud.

You may wish to have pupils who require a challenge write a poem about their family members and the kinds of jobs they do. Let pupils read their poems to the class.

9. Community Resources. Invite a parent or the school principal to tell the class about his or her work. Before the speaker arrives, help the class make up a list of questions to ask.

LESSON 4 PAGES 82–87

GOALS
1. To define *goods*. **2.** To understand that there are workers who produce goods. **3.** To name three goods used at home and three goods used in school.

READING VOCABULARY
goods

ORAL VOCABULARY
factory, assembly line

TEACHING SUGGESTIONS
1. Vocabulary Development. Ask pupils to name some things families buy in stores. (Food, clothes, toys, appliances, books) List the items on the chalkboard. Explain that these things are called *goods*. Help pupils develop the definition of goods as things that are made or grown.

2. Discussion. Review the list of goods from the last activity. Ask: *Where do stores get the goods they sell?* Allow pupils time to express themselves. Explain that most stores do not make the goods they sell. Most goods come from other places. This might be a good time to introduce the word *factory*. Write the word *factory* on the

chalkboard and ask pupils if they know what it means. Explain that a factory is a place where goods are made. Ask:

a. *Are there any factories in our community?*
b. *What goods are made in the factory?*
c. *What do factories do with the goods they make?*

3. Discussion. Start the discussion by saying the following: *People depend on factory workers for many goods. Without factory workers families could not have many of the goods they need and want. You depend on factory workers for many of the goods you use at home and in school.* Call on pupils to name some goods they use in school. (Pencils, crayons, books, paper)

4. Picture Reading. Tell the class that the pictures on pp. 82–87 tell the story of how crayons are made. Starting with p. 82, have pupils study the pictures while you read the text aloud. As pupils study the pictures, encourage them to ask questions about the pictures. Emphasize the help workers have from machines. The machine in the picture on p. 82 is a mixing vat. Liquid wax and the other ingredients are mixed together in the vat. Direct pupils' attention to the pictures at the top of p. 83. The picture on the left shows the wax being taken from the vat and poured into a molding machine to harden. The bottom picture shows a scraper removing all the extra wax. The hardened wax is now crayon. The crayons are raised out of the molds and put into holding trays. The crayons are now ready to be labeled. The picture on p. 85 shows a worker feeding the crayons into the labeling machine. The machine individually wraps each crayon according to color. After the crayons are labeled, different colored crayons are fed into another machine for packaging. Then the crayons are put into boxes. The boxes of crayons are shipped to many places. Ask:

a. *Why do workers produce goods?*

b. *Why do communities need workers?*
c. *What do workers do with the money they earn?*
5. Using a Map/Globe. Display a map of the United States and a globe. Collect packaging or boxes that tell where such items as pencils, pens, books, and crayons were made. Call on pupils to read the packaging to find out where the items were made and locate the places on the map or globe.

Now might be a good time to discuss transportation—how goods are sent from one place to another.

If pupils have a family member or neighbor who works in a factory, have them find out the kind of goods made and some of the places where the goods are sent. Find the places on a map or globe.

LESSON 5 PAGES 88–89

GOALS
1. To understand that there are workers who give or provide services. **2.** To define *services*. **3.** To understand that workers provide services to earn income.

READING VOCABULARY
services

TEACHING SUGGESTIONS
1. Discussion. Call on pupils to perform the following tasks:
a. *Erase the chalkboard.*
b. *Close the door.*
c. *Water the plant.*
d. *Clear off a table.*
Explain to the class that they have just performed services. Write the word *service* on the chalkboard. Define *service* as "the work people do for others." A service is "giving and receiving help." Ask the following questions:
a. *Do you help around the house?*

b. *What things can children help do?* (Dust, make beds, take out garbage)
2. Reading/Picture Reading. Have pupils turn to p. 88 and read the text silently. Call on pupils to read the text aloud. Ask a pupil to read the sentence that tells what services are.

Explain that people provide services to earn money. Focus attention on the picture. Explain that you, the teacher, provide a service and that you earn money for the work you do.

Focus attention on p. 89. Call on a pupil to read the first sentence aloud. Ask the following questions:
a. *How do the people in the pictures provide services?*
b. *Do they get paid for the work they do?*
c. *What do they do with the income they receive?*
d. *Name some other workers who provide a service.*
e. *Why do communities need service workers?*
f. *Do you know someone who provides a service?*
3. Research. Distribute magazines and have pupils find as many pictures as possible of workers who provide services. Have pupils show their pictures to the class and have the class guess the kinds of services the workers provide. Use the pictures to make a collage for the bulletin board. Label the collage "People in Communities Need Service Workers."

LESSON 6 PAGES 90–95

GOALS
1. To name two workers in the milk industry. **2.** To describe how milk gets from the dairy farm to stores. **3.** To name two products made from milk.

READING VOCABULARY
dairy farm

ORAL VOCABULARY
refrigerated

TEACHING SUGGESTIONS
1. Research. Distribute magazines and have pupils find as many pictures as they can showing a dairy farm or products made from milk. Help pupils arrange the pictures on a special bulletin-board display.

2. Discussion. Start a discussion about the importance of milk and milk products in our diet. Ask the following questions:

a. *What is a dairy farm?*

b. *What animals would you find on a dairy farm?* (Cows)

c. *Who works on a dairy farm?* (Farmer)

d. *What kinds of buildings would you find on a dairy farm?* (Barn, silo)

e. *What do dairy farmers raise?* (Cows)

f. *What do cows produce?* (Milk)

3. Picture Reading. Have pupils turn to pp. 90–91 and study the picture at the top of the page. Call on pupils to tell what they see.

Focus pupils' attention on the next picture. Ask: *What is going on in this picture?* Have pupils who have seen cows being milked to tell the class about it. Explain that cows were not always milked by machines. Long ago cows were milked by hand. Ask: *Why do you think farmers use machines to milk cows?* (Faster, more cows can be milked)

Have pupils turn to p. 92 and study the top picture. Ask the following questions:

a. *What does the farmer do with the milk?* (Sells it to a milk company)

b. *How does the milk get to the milk company?* (By truck)

c. *Who drives the truck?* (A truck driver)

d. *What kind of truck do you think this is?* (Refrigerated)

Call on a pupil to read the text under the top picture. Explain that a special kind of truck is used to carry the milk to the milk plant. Ask: *Why are refrigerated trucks used?* (So the milk won't spoil)

Have pupils look at the next picture on p. 92. Explain that there are many workers at the milk plant. They use machines to test the milk and make it safe to drink. Then the milk is packaged and bottled. Direct the pupils' attention to the picture on p. 93. Ask:

a. *What happens to milk after it is packaged?* (It is sold to stores.)

b. *How does the milk get to stores?* (By truck)

Focus pupils' attention on the picture on p. 94. Explain that after the milk is delivered to stores, workers sell the milk. Ask: *Who buys the milk?* (Families, people)

Call on a pupil to read the text on p. 95. Review with the class some of the workers needed to get milk from the farm to the table. (Farmer, truck driver, plant worker, delivery person, salesperson)

LESSON 7 PAGES 96–97

GOALS
1. To understand that when money is limited, people must choose what goods and services to buy. **2.** To define the word *save*. **3.** To understand the purpose of a budget.

READING VOCABULARY
choose, save, budget

ORAL VOCABULARY
penny, nickel, dime, quarter, half-dollar, dollar

TEACHING SUGGESTIONS
1. Discussion. Review with the class needs and wants discussed in this chapter. Help pupils conclude that some needs and wants are free (love, understanding, friends), but other needs and wants cost money (material things).

On the chalkboard write the words *penny, nickel, dime, quarter, and half-dollar.* Call on pupils to tell the number of cents each coin represents.

Review pupils' knowledge of the smaller denominations of paper money (one dollar, five dollars, and ten dollars).

2. Writing. Ask each pupil to fold a sheet of paper in half. On one half write the heading "goods." On the other half write "services." Have pupils list five goods and services they want or need.

Let pupils review their list and pick out the items they want most, in order of their priority.

Write the word *choose* on the chalkboard. Explain that when money is limited, families must choose what goods and services to buy.

3. Vocabulary Development. Write the word *save* on the chalkboard. Have pupils use the Glossary on pp. 182–183 to find the meaning. Tell pupils to read the last two sentences on p. 96. Ask the following questions:

a. *Can families always buy the things they want?*
b. *Does your family always buy the things it wants?*
c. *What do people do to get enough money?* (Save)

4. Picture Reading. Have pupils study the picture on p. 96 while you read the text aloud. Use the annotation at the bottom of the page to review pupils' knowledge of a bank.

5. Reading. Have pupils read the text on p. 97. Ask pupils if they know what the pie graph is for. Explain that the pie graph is a way of showing certain information. The graph on this page stands for a family's income. Read the last two sentences and have pupils answer the questions.

LESSON 8   PAGES 98–99

GOALS
1. To find Labor Day on a calendar. 2. To explain the meaning of Labor Day. 3. To use a dictionary to find the meaning of *recreation* and *relaxation*.

READING VOCABULARY
Labor Day
TEACHING SUGGESTIONS

1. Reading a Calendar. Display a calendar for September. Ask pupils if they know what special day is celebrated in September. Help the class discuss the purpose of Labor Day. Call on pupils to examine the calendar and tell what day Labor Day is celebrated. Explain that Labor Day is always celebrated on the first Monday in September.

2. Reading. Have pupils turn to p. 98 and read the text silently. Call on pupils to read aloud the sentences that answer the following questions:

a. *What do workers in our country do?*
b. *How do we feel about our jobs and workers?*
c. *When is Labor Day celebrated?*

3. Vocabulary Development. Write the words *recreation* and *relaxation* on the chalkboard. Have pupils find their definition in the dictionary. Call on volunteers to tell why they think workers need recreation and relaxation. Mention the importance of recreation and relaxation for maintaining good health. Have the class name some activities people do for recreation. Write the activities on the chalkboard. Mention that some people may do these same activities for work.

4. Picture Reading. Focus pupils attention on p. 99. Ask them to name the workers and speculate about the kind of work each person does. Ask if they know someone who does that kind of work.

3/CHAPTER REVIEW   PAGE 101
Answers for Review Questions
1. Something people must have to live.
2. Something people would like to have.
3. By working
4. Income
5. Answers will vary.
6. Labor Day
7. September

CHAPTER 4

Communities Make Rules

CHAPTER 4

COMMUNITIES MAKE RULES

Dear Parent,

We are now beginning Chapter 4 in our social studies textbook. This chapter will help your child understand the need for rules in the home, school, and community. Your child will learn how rules help people get along with one another, how rules help keep people safe and healthy, and how rules help protect people's rights and property.

In this chapter we will also be discussing community workers and the services they provide. Your child will learn about state and national leaders, the 50 states and their capital cities, and the President of our nation.

In connection with these topics, you may wish to discuss some rules that your family has and tell why they are necessary. Talk about some of the rules people are expected to obey in the school and community. Since children often feel that only they must follow rules, talk about some of the rules and laws that adults must also follow.

Thank you for your interest and assistance.

Sincerely,

COMMUNITIES MAKE RULES

THEME

People need rules and laws. Families, schools, and communities have rules. Leaders in our communities, towns, cities, states, and national government help make plans and laws for people to follow.

OVERVIEW

People need rules and laws to help them get along. Rules and laws give people rights and responsibilities. This chapter discusses family rules, school rules, and community rules. As pupils learn about rules at home and at school, they should understand more clearly the principles of rules and laws and their function in the community. The words *laws* and *rules* are often used interchangeably. In this chapter the pupils will learn that a law is a rule that people must obey.

BULLETIN–BOARD DISPLAY

Display the following pictures on the bulletin board:
1. A family watching TV, perhaps showing one person at the dial making a selection
2. A classroom scene showing children with their hands raised
3. A line of children waiting to board a school bus
4. Children putting some trash in a public trash can

GETTING STARTED

Discuss what is happening in each of the pictures displayed on the bulletin board. Ask: *What is a rule? Why do we have rules? What rules might a family have for selecting and watching television programs? Which of these rules would not be needed if a person lived alone? What are some of our rules at school? What rules would a classroom need when several children wish to speak at the same time? Why do people stand in line when waiting to get on a bus?*

LESSON 1   PAGES 106–109

GOALS

1. To know that rules help people get along with each other. **2.** To realize that rules protect the rights of the people in the community. **3.** To know that community rules are sometimes shown on signs. **4.** To name the signs pictured in the lesson and tell what they mean.

ORAL VOCABULARY

obeyed, handicapped

TEACHING SUGGESTIONS

1. Research Skills. Have the pupils locate the chapter title in the Contents at the front of their book. Ask: *On what page does this chapter begin? What is this chapter about?*

2. Reading Comprehension. After the pupils have read the first paragraph on p. 106, use the following questions to check their reading comprehension. *Who needs rules? Why do all people need rules to live by?* (Rules help people get along with one another, and they help to make sure that everyone is treated in a fair way.) *Do you think people have always had rules to live by? What makes you think so?*

3. Reading/Picture Reading. Have the pupils read the second paragraph on p. 106 and study the picture. Challenge the pupils to find as many examples as they can of ways that rules are being disobeyed.

Then have the pupils observe the picture on p. 107 and answer each of the questions asked at the top of the page. Ask: *How does following the rules make it easier for people to get along? Do you think this community made some new rules? How did the new rules help? How can you tell?*

4. Picture Reading/Discussion. As pictures are observed on pp. 108–109, ask: *Which of these signs are meant to help keep people safe in traffic? How do these signs help to keep people safe?* Point out

the sign for handicapped parking shown in the picture. Ask: *Have you seen this sign in your community? Why is this sign necessary?*

5. Group Work. Divide the class into four or five groups. Provide each group with a picture that shows a game being played or a group activity. Have each group talk about their picture and think of a rule that relates to the game or activity shown in the picture. Ask each group to share their picture and rule with the class. As each group presents their picture and rule, write the rule on the chalkboard and allow time for class discussion. Select one or two pupils to put each picture and corresponding rule into a class booklet. Ask pupils to provide ideas for the title of the booklet.

LESSON 2   PAGES 110–111

GOALS

1. To know that it is important for families to have rules. **2.** To name some rules that families have to help them get along. **3.** To name some rules that help keep families safe and healthy. **4.** To explain why families have rules.

ORAL VOCABULARY

safety

TEACHING SUGGESTIONS

1. Thinking Skills. Review Lesson 1 with the pupils, pointing out that all people need rules to live by. Ask: *Where do we first learn about following rules?* (Home and family) *Can you think of a rule you follow at home? Who made the rule? How does this rule help you? Do you always try to follow the rule? What happens when you forget to follow one of the rules at home? What rule at home do you least like? Why is that rule important? What rules at home were made to help keep you safe?* Through the discussion, help the pupils discover why they must follow rules at home; help them realize that parents, too, follow rules.

2. Reading Comprehension/Picture Reading. Select pupils to read the lesson on p. 110 aloud. Ask the pupils to name some of the reasons why families have rules. Ask: *What family rules are talked about on p. 110?* Have pupils observe the pictures on pp. 110–111 and answer the questions presented in the lesson. Ask: *Why is it important for family members to follow safety rules? What are some of the safety rules you and your family follow at home? What safety rules do you follow away from home?*

3. Discussion/Vocabulary Development. To enrich the pupils' understanding of the words *health* and *safety*, promote a class discussion based on these questions: *How do you feel when you are healthy? How do you feel when you are not healthy?* Help the pupils understand that healthy people are people who are not sick or injured; they feel well; and they are generally happier and can do more things than people who are not healthy. Ask: *What does it mean to be safe? What are some of the ways to be safe on the playground? In the classroom? In the swimming pool? On a bicycle?* Point out to the pupils that people can try to keep safe by following safety rules.

4. Picture Reading. Ask the pupils to identify the pictures on pp. 110–111 that show health rules being followed. Refer to the picture on the bottom of p. 111 and ask: *What is this child doing to stay healthy?* Direct the pupils to observe the picture at the top of p. 110 and ask: *What is this girl doing to keep her teeth healthy? What else can you do to keep healthy teeth?* (See a dentist for a regular checkup.) *How does a dentist help to keep your teeth healthy?*

Call attention to the picture on the top of p. 111 showing a family cleaning the room. Ask the pupils if they can tell from the picture if this family has rules about sharing the work. Ask: *What rules do you think these family members are following?* Dis-

cuss the rules mentioned by the pupils. *How is each person helping? Which of these rules do you follow at home? Does your family have rules about what jobs people do?* Allow the pupils to share their family rules with the class.

● **5. Research.** Write several safety topics on 3″ × 5″ index cards. Example:

a. Being safe on the playground

b. Being safe while riding a bike

c. Being safe while skating

d. Being safe around animals

e. Being safe at home

f. Being safe around water

Divide the class into five or six groups. Allow each group to choose a topic and find or draw pictures to show what the topic is about. For those pupils who need a challenge, ask them to write three safety rules about the topic they have selected.

LESSON 3   PAGES 112–113

GOALS

1. To name three kinds of school rules.
2. To name three library rules. **3.** To name three fire-drill safety rules.

ORAL VOCABULARY
fire drill

TEACHING SUGGESTIONS

1. Discussion. Explain to the pupils that school workers and pupils are responsible for making good rules for the school. Ask: *What school worker is responsible for the rules for the whole school? Who is responsible for our classroom rules? For whom are most of the rules made?* (Everybody)

2. Reading Comprehension. After the pupils have read the lesson text on p. 112, ask them to name three kinds of rules that are used at school. (Playing, learning, and safety) Ask a volunteer to read p. 112 aloud. Guide the discussion as pupils answer the question on p. 112.

3. Picture Reading. Call attention to the picture on the top of p. 112. Ask: *Can you tell what game these children might be playing?* Point out that rules must be followed when games are played. Ask: *What rules do you think these children are following?* Write their responses on the chalkboard. Ask: *What might happen if these rules were not followed? How do rules help on the playground?* (They help everyone get a turn.) Direct the pupils to observe the picture at the bottom of p. 112 and ask: *Why do we need library rules? What kind of rules are needed in the library? What rules do you follow in the library? How does the librarian know who has a book?* After pupils have read p. 113, direct them to observe the picture at the top of the page. Ask: *What rules are these children following in the classroom? What might happen if these children did not raise their hand before talking? How would it sound if everyone talked at the same time? What rules are followed during a fire drill? What might happen if there were no fire drills?* The picture at the bottom of p. 113 shows a list of fire-drill safety rules. Ask for a volunteer to read these rules.

4. Discussion. Discuss how politeness is a part of obeying rules. Ask: *When do you use the words "please" and "thank you"? When are you supposed to say "pardon me"? "Excuse me"? Why should we always try to be polite? How do you feel when someone is rude to you?* Talk about some rules that are a part of politeness. (Rules about sharing, taking turns, and listening to directions)

LESSON 4   PAGES 114–115

GOALS

1. To know that people who work follow rules. **2.** To know that some rules help keep people safe and healthy. **3.** To name three health and safety rules being followed by the workers shown in the lesson pictures.

4. To know that some jobs have special rules.

ORAL VOCABULARY
health workers

TEACHING SUGGESTIONS

1. Reading Comprehension. After the pupils have read pp. 114–115, discuss why rules are important to people who work. Ask the pupils to give two ways that rules help workers. (Rules help people work together and keep people safe and healthy.) Discuss the question asked on p. 115.

2. Picture Reading. Call attention to the pictures on pp. 114–115. Ask: *Which of these pictures shows people following health rules? What kind of health rules are being followed? Why is the doctor wearing a mask? How will the mask help the doctor to be safe? Which of these pictures shows people following safety rules? What are the workers on the tall building doing? What are the workers doing to keep safe? What might happen if the workers did not follow special safety rules?*

3. Thinking Skills. Say: *There are many different kinds of workers. Many workers have jobs to help keep people healthy. These people are called health workers.* Ask: *In what ways do you think health workers help people stay healthy? Who are some of the health workers you know about?* Point out that some people have the job of helping others to be safe. Ask: *What do you think these workers are called? Are there any busy streets near your school? Does a safety worker help you cross the street? What other kinds of safety workers can you think of?*

4. Art. Ask the pupils to draw some pictures of things that make warning sounds and help us to be safe. (Fire truck, police car, ambulance, train, lifeguard with whistle) Display the pictures in the classroom using the caption "Sounds Help Us to Be Safe."

GOALS

1. To know that rules and laws are needed in the community. **2.** To define *laws*. **3.** To name some rules and laws that are made by the community. **4.** To name two ways that laws help people in the community.

READING VOCABULARY

laws

ORAL VOCABULARY

litter, no trespassing

TEACHING SUGGESTIONS

1. Speaking Skills. Help the pupils recall some rules made in the home and some rules made in the school. Ask: *Why are rules necessary in the home and in the school?*

2. Vocabulary Development. Write the vocabulary word *laws* on the chalkboard. Ask: *What do you think this word means?* Direct the pupils to the Glossary in the back of their book. Ask for a volunteer to read the definition of *law*. Help the pupils understand that some rules are called laws.

3. Discussion. Explain to the pupils that communities make rules. These rules are called laws. Communities have laws to help and protect the people and the things people own. Ask: *What do you think would happen if there were no rules for the classroom, the playground, or a community?*

4. Picture Reading. Direct the pupils' attention to the picture of a sign saying "No Trespassing" on p. 116. Ask if anyone can read the words on the sign. Ask: *What does trespassing mean? Have you ever seen a sign like this? Why would someone put a sign like this on their property? What do you think might happen if someone goes on this property? Would they be breaking the law?*

Discuss the meaning of the word *fine*. Have the pupils find the sign that uses the word *fine*. Discuss the offense of littering. Ask: *Does our community have a law to stop littering? Are there any signs in our community about littering?*

Direct the pupils' attention to the picture on p. 117. Ask: *What law do you think the driver of this car has broken? How is this police officer seeing that the law is obeyed? What responsibility might the driver of this car have for the ticket?*

5. Interview. Have each pupil ask a parent about the safety rules at the place where he or she works. Instruct the pupils to have their parent write down one safety rule. Have pupils bring these to class. Discuss the different safety rules collected and the reason for each rule.

6. Experience Charts. Divide the class into groups. Assign one of the following tasks to each group. Make a list of rules for the following:

a. Rules for the library
b. Rules for the playground
c. Rules for the park

GOALS

1. To tell how community leaders are chosen. **2.** To tell why communities need leaders. **3.** Identify two ways in which the mayor helps people in the community. **4.** To define *taxes*.

READING VOCABULARY

taxes

ORAL VOCABULARY

secret ballot, council, commissioner, government, election

TEACHING SUGGESTIONS

1. Picture Reading/Thinking Skills. Call

attention to the voting booth in the picture on the top of p. 118. Point out to the pupils that people vote to elect community leaders on Election Day. People vote on a secret ballot. Ask: *What does secret mean? Have you ever kept a secret from someone?* Say: *When people vote on a secret ballot, this means the vote is a secret. The person with the most votes becomes the community leader.* Ask: *Do you think people should use secret ballots when they vote? Why or why not?*

2. Reading Comprehension. After the pupils have read p. 118 ask: *How do the people elect community leaders? How do leaders help people in the community? How does the mayor help the community?* Ask the pupils to find the paragraph on p. 118 that tells about the mayor. Ask for a volunteer to read this paragraph aloud. Ask the students if they know the name of their city mayor and if they know where the mayor's office is located. Discuss the fact that the mayor of a city is elected by the people of the city.

3. Discussion. Explain to the pupils that the mayor cannot do all of the work in a community. Other leaders are chosen to help. These community leaders help decide what services the community needs. Leaders make and carry out laws and rules that help to protect the people and their goods. The leaders help to decide what services the community needs. Ask: *Who are some of the leaders that help the mayor?* You may wish to introduce the terms *city council* or *commissioners* at this time and discuss these jobs. Explain to the pupils that the plan for running a community is called its government.

4. Picture Reading. Call attention to the picture of the city council on p. 118. Ask: *What does this picture show?* Point out that this picture shows a city council meeting. Ask: *How do you think these people were chosen? What kind of decisions might these leaders have to make?*

5. Reading Comprehension. After pupils have read p. 119, use the following questions to check their reading comprehension and to promote class discussion. Ask: *How does the community receive money? What is this money called? How is tax money used? How are community workers paid? How do community workers make the community a better place to live?* Ask the pupils to speculate about what might happen if their community did not have community workers.

6. Picture Reading. Direct the pupils' attention to the picture on p. 119. Point out that this person is paying money to the community. Have pupils look at the sign in the picture. Ask: *What is money paid to the community called?* Be sure that pupils understand the meaning of *tax.* (A *tax* is "money paid by people to support their community.") Help them understand that the money spent by the community leaders comes from the taxes people pay. Ask: *Why do you think community leaders need tax money? How do you think the community leaders might decide to use tax money?*

LESSON 7   PAGES 120–121

GOALS
1. To know that elected leaders in each state help make plans and laws for the state. **2.** To define *governor*. **3.** To know that each state has a capital city. **4.** To tell where laws and plans for the state are made. **5.** To name the capital of Tennessee. **6.** To locate Nashville on a map.

READING VOCABULARY
governor, capital city

TEACHING SUGGESTIONS
1. Discussion. Review with the pupils some characteristics of cities and towns. Ask the pupils to tell what large cities, small cities, and towns are like. Review

with the pupils why people who live and work together need rules. Point out that one town or city cannot make plans and laws for others. Ask: *Who, do you think, makes the laws for a state?*

2. Reading Comprehension. After the pupils have read the lesson on pp. 120–121, ask: *How do people choose leaders to help make plans and laws for the state? What is the leader of a state called?* (Governor) *How does a person become a governor? Where are the laws for the state made?*

3. Map Reading. Direct the pupils to look at the map on p. 121. Ask: *What does this map show?* (The state of Tennessee) *What is the capital of Tennessee?* (Nashville) *How is the capital shown on the map?* (Star symbol) *Why do you think Nashville is a good location for the state capital?*

4. Map Skills. Use a United States classroom map to point out the state of Tennessee to the pupils. Ask: *Is Tennessee located in the eastern or western part of the United States?* Ask the pupils to name the states bordering Tennessee. Then have the pupils use the map on p. 121 to locate the Tennessee River. *Does this river run through Nashville? In what state do we live?* Ask for a volunteer to locate your state on the United States map. *Is our state near or far away from the state of Tennessee?*

LESSON 8 PAGES 122–123

GOALS

1. To know that the United States has 50 states. **2.** To name and locate the capital of your state. **3.** To determine directions from a particular state to another.

ORAL VOCABULARY
border

TEACHING SUGGESTIONS

1. Map Skills/Writing Skills. Review with the pupils the role of maps in helping to locate places. Help the pupils locate their home state on a classroom United States map. Ask them to name and locate the capital city. Write the name of the capital city on the chalkboard. Have the pupils write the name of the state and capital city on their paper. Then ask them to select five more states and write those state names and capital cities on their paper.

2. Reading Comprehension/Map Skills. After the pupils have read the lesson on pp. 122–123, ask: *Our country is made up of how many states? What does the map in this lesson show?* (The map shows the 50 states of our country and each state capital.) *How are the states identified on the map?* (Large bold print) *How is the name of the capital city identified on the map?* (A star identifies the capital city.)

3. Vocabulary Development. Introduce the term *border*. Tell the pupils that the line between their state and the state next to it is a border. Explain that the land on one side of the border belongs to their state and the land on the other side of the border belongs to the other state. Have the pupils use the map on pp. 122–123 to locate the states that border their state.

4. Finding Directions. Write the following states on the chalkboard: South Dakota, California, Virginia, and Texas. Ask the pupils to look at the map on pp. 122–123 and locate the state of Kansas. Have pupils tell which direction they would travel from Kansas to each of the four states.

5. Map Reading. Ask the pupils to observe the map on pp. 122–123 in their text. Ask:
a. *Which state is the largest?*
b. *Name the state that is farthest west.*
c. *Name the three states that touch California.*
d. *Name four states that begin with the letter M.*
● **6. Research/Writing Skills.** Have the pupils pretend they are going to visit one of the states listed below. Help them write a story telling how they would get there, what they might do there, and things they

might see. For those pupils who need a challenge, ask them to find out what goods are produced in these states:
Texas, New York, Alaska, Florida, California, Michigan

LESSON 9   PAGES 124–125

GOALS

1. To know that members of Congress are elected by the people of their state. 2. To know that laws for all the states are made by Congress. 3. To know that the leader of our country is the President. 4. To name the President. 5. To name our national capital. 6. To know that the President lives and works in Washington, D.C.

READING VOCABULARY

Congress, President

ORAL VOCABULARY

White House, District of Columbia, government, fair

TEACHING SUGGESTIONS

1. **Vocabulary Development.** Write the word *Washington, D.C.,* on the chalkboard. Ask the pupils if they know what *D.C.* stands for. Explain that it stands for "District of Columbia" and that the city is not in a state but in a special district. It is on land set aside for the country's capital. Write *capital* and *Capitol* on the chalkboard. Explain to the pupils the difference between these two words. (One refers to the city and the other refers to the building where the lawmakers meet.) Write the words *President* and *Congress* on the chalkboard. Pronounce the words and mention that the President and members of Congress are leaders for our country. Direct the pupils to read the lesson on pp. 124–125 to find out what these leaders do.

2. **Map Skills.** On a large map of the United States help the pupils locate Washington, D.C. Discuss the location of Washington, D.C., in relation to your state.

3. **Reading Comprehension/Discussion.** Ask the pupils to read p. 124 silently. Ask: *Who picks the leaders for Congress? Who is the leader of our country?* Have one pupil read aloud all the sentences that tell about the President. Ask: *Who elects the President? What does the President do? What is the President's name?* Direct the pupils to the picture on p. 124 and ask them to identify the President pictured (Ronald Wilson Reagan). Have the pupils read the last part of the lesson on p. 125 and tell where our country's leaders work. Ask: *What is the capital of our country? What does national capital mean?* (Explain that our country is a union of 50 states that make up our nation and that Washington, D.C., is the head city.) Mention that the capital is the center of government for our country. Ask: *Where does the President live and work?*

4. **Picture Reading.** Call attention to the picture of the Capitol on p. 125. Ask: *What is this building used for?* (It is used as a meeting place for leaders of the United States.)

Have the pupils look again at the aerial view picture of Washington, D.C., on p. 125. Direct their attention to the other buildings that can be identified. Stress that Washington, D.C., is our national capital and that it is a very special city. Elicit from students the meaning of *special*. Encourage them to speculate about why Washington is a special city. Tell them that there are many memorials in Washington, D.C., that remind us of great people and events in our country's history.

5. **Making a Model.** Help the pupils make a model of the capital city on a table in the classroom. Use a map of Washington, D.C., as a guide for building locations. You may wish to have the pupils use small boxes to represent some of the buildings and monuments.

6. **Story Hour.** Read *Our Nation's Capital: Washington, D.C.,* by Bernadine Bailey.

CHAPTER 5
Communities Long Ago and Today

CHAPTER 5

COMMUNITIES LONG AGO AND TODAY

Dear Parent,

    Your child is starting a new chapter in *Neighborhoods and Communities* called "Communities Long Ago and Today."

    This chapter is about the history of our country. We will learn how the Native Americans and the colonists met their basic needs for food, clothes, and shelter. We will also learn how communities in our country have grown and changed.

    To prepare your child for this chapter, you might like to explore your own family history or the history of your community. If you have pictures of a restored colonial town, a Native American village, or the site of an early settlement, you might want to show these pictures to your child. If your community has a museum or historical society, you might also want to take your child for a visit.

    Thank you for helping your child understand more fully the history of our country.

                         Sincerely,

COMMUNITIES LONG AGO AND TODAY

THEME

People have always lived in communities. Communities long ago served the same purposes as they do today.

OVERVIEW

This chapter focuses on the history of our country. Pupils will learn about the first Americans, about communities long ago, and about the ways in which basic needs were met.

Pupils will also learn about the first English colonists who came to America.

As comparisons are made between our country long ago and today, pupils will discover some of the many ways America has grown and changed.

BULLETIN-BOARD DISPLAY

Collect and display pictures. Make a bulletin board entitled "Communities Long Ago and Today." Display pictures showing how Indians and colonists' families lived long ago and how families live today. Some "long ago" pictures may be obtained from the local Chamber of Commerce. Include family portraits as well as houses, stores, and farms.

GETTING STARTED

Help pupils compile a brief history about their community. Begin by posing the following questions and using the library or community resources to find the answers:
a. When was the community started?
b. How did it get its name?
c. What are the oldest buildings?
d. What are the oldest businesses or industries? When did they begin?
e. When was the first school built?

You might also have pupils ask a parent or older citizen for information about the community. Help pupils understand that this kind of information is their community's history.

LESSON 1 PAGES 132–133

GOALS

1. To develop an understanding of some of the history of our country. 2. To define *wilderness*. 3. To identify the first Americans. 4. To describe how our country looked when only the Indians lived here. 5. To name some things communities today have that communities long ago did not have.

READING VOCABULARY
wilderness

ORAL VOCABULARY
canoe, bow and arrow, natural features

TEACHING SUGGESTIONS

1. **Reading.** Ask pupils, *What do you know about our country's history?* Have them read the text on pp. 132–133. Show pictures of the natural and physical features of our country (mountains, fields, plains and forests). Tell pupils to imagine a large area without stores, highways, or skyscrapers. Explain that about 350 years ago most of our country was a wilderness. On the chalkboard write the definition of *wilderness* as a place that has not been changed by people.

2. **Picture Reading/Discussion.** Call attention to the picture on pp. 132–133. Ask the following questions to generate a discussion:

a. *Who are the people shown in the picture?*

b. *What are they doing?*

c. *What is the name of the boat? What was it used for?*

d *Where do you think they live?*

e. *What is the bow and arrow used for?*

Explain that Indians were once the only people living in the United States.

3. **Using a Map.** Tell pupils that long ago Indians lived all over the United States.

Display a large wall map of the United States. Point out the regions where different tribes or groups lived. Make labels using such groups as Pueblo, Navajo, Seminole, and Iroquois. Tape the labels to the appropriate parts of the map. (Pueblo—southwest; Navajo—northwest; Seminole—southeast; and Iroquois—northeast)

LESSON 2 PAGES 134–135

GOALS

1. To understand that the Indians lived in groups called tribes. 2. To define *village*. 3. To name two kinds of houses built by Indians long ago and describe how they were built.

READING VOCABULARY
village

ORAL VOCABULARY
handmade, natural resources

TEACHING SUGGESTIONS

1. **Picture Reading.** Have pupils turn to p. 134 and describe what they see. Ask:

a. *What is the man carrying?*

b. *Where do you think he is going?*

c. *Describe the clothes the Indians are wearing.*

d. *What are the round buildings?* (Houses)

e. *What are the buildings made of?* (Trees)

Explain that everything used by the Indians was handmade. They used the natural resources of the area where they lived. Natural resources are things that are not made by people.

2. **Discussion.** Have pupils read the text on pp. 134–135. Define *village* as a small community with few people, houses, and other buildings. Ask:

a. *What do these pictures tell about how the Indians lived?*

b. *How did they meet their need for food?*

For clothes? For shelter?

c. *If there were no schools, how did Indian children learn?* (From parents and from adult members of the tribe)

3. Picture Reading. To help pupils conclude that Indians used the natural resources of the area in which they lived, focus attention on the wigwam, p. 134. Explain that a wigwam was made from young green trees. One end of a tree was bent over and stuck deep in the ground. Then the other end was put in the ground to make an arch. Wide strips of bark were tied to the frame to make walls. A hole was cut in the roof to let fire smoke out.

4. Picture Reading. Focus pupils' attention on the pueblo. Ask: *How are they like today's apartment buildings?* Explain that Pueblo is also the name of the Indian tribes that built these houses. Pueblos were made from blocks of mud shaped and dried. They were built one on top of the other. Each group of pueblos was like a single village. Ask: *Why do you think the Pueblo Indians made their homes from mud?* (There were few trees where they lived.)

5. Picture Reading. Call on a pupil to read the last sentence on p. 135. Explain that these cone-shaped houses were called tepees. Many Plains Indians lived in tepees. Since the Plains Indians were hunters, they were constantly following the animals they hunted for food. They needed houses that were easy to put up and take down. They built tepees by placing long poles in a circle. The poles were tied together at the top. Then animal skins were stretched over the poles. A flap at the top of the tepee allowed smoke to go out.

6. Research. Make a large information chart. Have pupils find pictures of pottery, baskets, fabric weaving, and other items made by Indians. Ask pupils to bring to class items they may have at home that are related to Indian life.

• **7. Art.** Help pupils make placemats from pieces of yarn or construction paper. You may wish to have pupils who require a challenge make a model of a tepee. To make a model of a tepee, get 12 sticks about a foot long and strip off the bark. Cross two of the sticks about an inch from the top and tie them together. Tie the remaining 10 sticks to the first two, making a cone-shaped circular frame. Use a piece of cloth to cover the frame. Leave an opening flap for a door and also an opening at the top.

LESSON 3   PAGES 136–137

GOALS

1. To name and describe the kind of houses made by the Iroquois. **2.** To compare and contrast a longhouse with other types of houses built by Indians. **3.** To understand that all Indians used available natural resources to build their homes.

READING VOCABULARY
longhouse

ORAL VOCABULARY
woodland

TEACHING SUGGESTIONS

1. Reading for Information. Ask the pupils to silently read the text on pp. 136–137. Then call on a pupil to read aloud the part of the text that answers the following questions.

a. *What kind of houses did the Iroquois build?*

b. *Why was a tall fence built around the village?*

c. *How did the Iroquois meet their need for food?*

2. Discussion. Explain that the Iroquois were also called Woodland Indians because they lived in the forests of upstate New York. If you did not do so in Lesson 1, make a label for the Iroquois and attach it to the United States map. Ask:

a. *How do you think the longhouse got its name?*

b. *How did the longhouse differ from the homes of other groups?*

c. *What did the Iroquois use to build their homes?*

d. *In what ways do people today use trees?*

3. Art. Give each pupil a sheet of drawing paper. Have them fold the paper into four equal parts. Tell them to look at the pictures on pp. 134–137 and make a drawing of each of the houses shown. Have pupils label each house and display the drawings on the classroom wall or in a booklet.

4. Art. Explain that Indians used drums and smoke signals to communicate over long distances. Have pupils make drums from oatmeal boxes. Cover the boxes with construction paper and decorate them with drawings and paintings of Indian designs.

5. Reading. Have pupils read the text on p. 137. Reinforce the understanding that most Indian families did everything for themselves.

LESSON 4   PAGES 138–139

GOALS

1. To use a globe to trace the route of the colonists from England to America. **2.** To define *settlement*. **3.** To name the first permanent English settlement in America. **4.** To identify Virginia as the part of America where Jamestown was built. **5.** To locate Virginia on a map of the United States.

READING VOCABULARY
Atlantic Ocean, settlement

ORAL VOCABULARY
settlers

TEACHING SUGGESTIONS

1. Discussion. Ask the pupils to make believe their families are going to move to a place far away. List on the chalkboard all the things that they would want to carry to the new home. Then explain that all these things may be too heavy. Go back and cross off all but the essentials. After pupils have shared ideas, tell them that long ago the colonists actually left their home and traveled across the sea to find a new home. They had to make decisions just like the one the class made.

Give a brief history of the colonists by asking: *Did you ever wish for a place where you could do all the things you wanted to do? What would that place be like?* People long ago had many of the same wishes that people have today. Long ago some people in England wanted a new home. They left England in three small ships and sailed to America. They were the first English colonists or settlers to come to live in the United States. Use the annotations at the top and bottom of p. 139 to help pupils understand that the English colonists were not the first people to settle in America.

2. Using a Globe. Display a classroom globe and help pupils locate England and the United States. Call on pupils to name the ocean the colonists crossed.

3. Reading for Information. Have pupils read the lesson on p. 139 and answer the following:

a. *Which country did the colonists come from?*

b. *Why did they come to our country?*

c. *Why did they name their settlement Jamestown?*

d. *Where was the community of Jamestown built?*

LESSON 5   PAGES 140–141

GOALS

1. To define *fort* and describe its use. **2.** To identify a log cabin as one type of house built by the colonists. **3.** To understand that children long ago learned from their parents and shared the work. **4.** To arrange sentences in sequential order.

READING VOCABULARY
fort, protection

ORAL VOCABULARY
defense

TEACHING SUGGESTIONS
1. Discussion. Have pupils turn to p. 140 and study the picture while you read the text aloud. Direct attention to the various buildings in the fort and discuss what they were like. Have pupils make guesses about each building's use.
2. Vocabulary Development. Write the words *fort* and *protection* on the chalkboard. Define *fort* as a building or place that provides defense and protection.
3. Understanding Sequence. Write the following sentences on the chalkboard and have pupils number the sentences in the order in which they happened.
The colonists built a fort. (4)
The colonists left England. (1)
The colonists crossed the Atlantic Ocean. (2)
The colonists landed at Jamestown, Virginia. (3)
4. Discussion. Have pupils read the text on p. 141. Explain that the settlement of Jamestown started to grow. Colonists started building houses in the forests. Ask: *What did they use to build their homes?* (Wood) *Is wood a natural resource?* Display pictures of the interior of a log cabin. Point out that the colonists had to make many of their own things. Children had to help share the work. Tell pupils to study the picture. Ask: *What are these children doing? What will the wood be used for?*

Discuss the clothes the children are wearing. Have pupils compare colonists' clothes with clothes worn by the Indians.
● **5. Art.** Have pupils make a mural showing colonists and their homes. They might include forest animals, such as deer, raccoons, and wild turkeys.

You may wish to have pupils who require a challenge use library resources to find out more about ways the first colonists lived and make an oral report to the class.
6. Story Hour. Read to the class *Getting to Know Jamestown* by Buck Davis.

LESSON 6 PAGES 142–143

GOALS
1. To name the second oldest English settlement in America. **2.** To find Massachusetts on a map of the United States. **3.** To tell one way the Indians helped the colonists. **4.** To understand the meaning of the first Thanksgiving celebration.

READING VOCABULARY
survive, Thanksgiving

ORAL VOCABULARY
tradition, harvest

TEACHING SUGGESTIONS
1. Discussion. Start a discussion with the following: *After the settlement at Jamestown another group of colonists left England for America. These colonists were called Pilgrims. They started a settlement in Plymouth, in what is now the state of Massachusetts. It was almost winter when the Pilgrims arrived at Plymouth. The weather was cold, and they did not have much food. The Pilgrims had a hard time their first year.*

Ask: *What problems do you think the Pilgrims had?* Help the pupils understand that the colonists in Plymouth had problems similar to those experienced by the colonists in Jamestown. The weather was very cold, and they didn't have enough food. *Who do you think helped the Pilgrims to survive that first year?* (The Indians)
2. Using a Map/Globe. Display a United States map or a classroom globe. Have pupils locate Massachusetts. Ask:

a. In what part of the U.S. is Massachusetts located?

b. What direction is Massachusetts from your community?

c. What ocean did the colonists cross to reach Massachusetts?

3. Reading for Information. Have pupils read silently the text on p. 142. Then call on pupils to read aloud the sentences that answer the following:

a. What was the name of the second oldest settlement?

b. Where was the settlement built?

c. How did the Indians help the colonists? Discuss answers to questions, stressing the helpfulness of the Indians. If possible, find some pictures of the reconstructed Pilgrim village at Plimoth Plantation in Massachusetts.

4. Discussion/Picture Reading. Call attention to the picture on p. 143. Have pupils tell what they know about the first Thanksgiving. Ask: What people do you see in this picture? What are they doing? What special day does this picture show? Write the words harvest and Thanksgiving on the chalkboard. Have pupils read the text on p. 143. Explain that the first Thanksgiving in our country was celebrated by the Pilgrims and the Indians. The Pilgrims were thankful for their new home, their health, and their abundant harvest. Define harvest as a time when crops are picked or gathered. The Pilgrims were also thankful for the help given them by the Indians.

LESSON 7 PAGES 144–145

GOALS

1. To name the first two English settlements in America. **2.** To name special kinds of work colonists did. **3.** To name two things children long ago learned in school. **4.** To describe some materials used for learning long ago.

READING VOCABULARY
teacher, carpenter, tinsmith

ORAL VOCABULARY
specialize, hornbook, primer

TEACHING SUGGESTIONS

1. Vocabulary Development. Review with the class how the first colonists met their basic needs. Explain that as communities grew and changed, the ways in which people met their needs changed. Write the word specialize on the chalkboard. Define specialize as doing a particular kind of work.

2. Reading. Call on pupils to read the text on p. 144 to find other special kinds of work the colonists did. Make a list on the chalkboard. Add jobs such as teaching, iron making, coopering, glass making, and blacksmithing to the list. Discuss each job with the class.

3. Picture Reading. Have pupils study the picture on p. 144. Discuss the activities going on in the classroom as well as the materials being used. Explain that when the colonists first came to America, there were no schools. Children were taught at home. Then later, as communities grew, schools were built. The picture on p. 144 shows how the first classrooms looked. Ask: What do you think children learned in schools long ago? (Reading, writing, spelling, and arithmetic) Do you learn the same things in schools today? What other things do you learn?

As pupils observe the picture, explain that children long ago did not have many books. There were no chalkboards or maps. Usually the class had only hornbooks. Hornbooks consisted of a sheet of paper made from ox horns. The hornbooks were used for learning the alphabet and for practicing printing. Some children had books called primers. A primer was a small book for teaching children to read.

4. Spelling Match. Tell pupils they are

going to play a game that children long ago played in school. Have pupils form two lines at the front of the room. Using simple words from this or previous lessons, call on a pupil in the first line to spell a word. If the pupil cannot spell the word, he or she must return to their seat, and a child from the other line is asked to spell the word. Continue the spelling match until only one child is left standing.

5. Picture Reading. Call attention to the carpenter on p. 145. Ask:

a. *What is this worker called?*

b. *What piece of furniture is shown in the picture?*

c. *What do carpenters today do?*

d. *How is their work today different from the work of carpenters in the early days?*

Continue with similar questions for the picture of the tinsmith. Help pupils conclude that as communities grew and changed, people began doing special work.

6. Story Hour. Read to the class *Life in Colonial Times* by Elizabeth G. Speare.

7. Following Directions. Choose sentences from the story and write them on the chalkboard. Have pupils draw a line under the sentences that are true about colonial life; for example:

1. *Long ago colonists came to this country.*

2. *They came across the sea in an airplane.*

3. *Indians came with the colonists.*

4. *The colonists had a hard time during their first year in this country.*

LESSON 8 PAGES 146–147

GOALS

1. To compare and contrast communities long ago with communities today. **2.** To understand that communities change to meet the needs of their people.

READING VOCABULARY
rural, suburb

ORAL VOCABULARY
construction

TEACHING SUGGESTIONS

1. Discussion. Begin a discussion by asking pupils how they have changed in the last few years. Explain that most communities also change. Ask the class to name some ways communities change; then write their responses on the chalkboard. (By building roads and bridges, by replacing old buildings with new ones, by making parks and playgrounds)

2. Field Trip. Find out if new construction is going on in the community. Have the class visit the construction site. When pupils return to the classroom have them discuss possible reasons for the construction.

3. Reading for Information. Have pupils turn to p. 146 and read the text. Call on pupils to read the sentences that answer the following:

a. *What kinds of communities do families live in today?*

b. *How did people long ago meet their needs for clothes?*

c. *How do people today get food?*

d. *What did people long ago use to build their homes?*

Have pupils read the text on p. 147 and answer the question.

4. Picture Reading. Have pupils study the pictures on pp. 146–147. Tell the class that the two pictures were drawn by an artist. The first pictures shows a street many years ago. The second picture shows the same street as it looks today. Ask pupils to find as many things as they can that have changed.

5. Research. Assign or have pupils choose one way in which life in communities has changed. Choose things such as transportation, clothing, housing, communication, and stores. Have pupils find pictures or make drawings of these changes.

You may wish to have pupils who require a challenge write a story about the topic they chose.

6. Poetry. Have pupils turn back to pp. 130–131 and study the picture as you read the poem aloud. Call on pupils to read one or two lines of the poem aloud.

LESSON 9   PAGES 148–151

GOALS
1. To understand that some communities have people with similar backgrounds.
2. To understand that some communities have people with diverse backgrounds.
3. To understand that all people have customs and traditions. **4.** To name a custom their family follows.

READING VOCABULARY
background

ORAL VOCABULARY
culture, custom, ancestors

TEACHING SUGGESTIONS
1. Reading. Display a large map of the world. Read aloud the first two paragraphs on p. 148. On the map point out the places mentioned in the text. Help pupils conclude that people have come from almost every place on earth to live in the United States.

2. Vocabulary Development. Introduce and develop the meaning of the words *background, culture,* and *custom.* Have pupils read the last paragraph on p. 148. Guide pupils toward the understanding that culture is a way of living, doing, thinking, believing. Ask: *Did the Indians and colonists have the same customs? What things were different?* (Food, language, clothes, houses, and tools) Help pupils conclude that the Indians and colonists

had different cultures and that customs differ from one culture to another.

3. Discussion. To further help pupils understand that Americans come from many cultural backgrounds and have different customs, write the names of some holidays on the chalkboard. Include national, traditional, and ethnic holidays. Call out the name of each holiday and give a brief significance of each. Ask:
a. *What do people do on holidays?*
b. *Do you celebrate this holiday?*
c. *Does everyone in the class celebrate this holiday?*
d. *Do people in other parts of the world celebrate this holiday?*
e. *Why do we have holidays?*
f. *Do all people celebrate the same holidays? Why not?*

4. Reading for Information. Have pupils read the text on p. 148 and name two things that may differ from one culture to another. *What other things might be different?* (Music, dance, games, and holidays)

5. Group Work. Plan a party with the class. Have pupils wear traditional costumes and sing songs and do dances from other cultures. Bring in foods from different cultures for pupils to sample.

6. Art. Have pupils draw a picture showing a family custom.

7. Reading/Discussion. Have pupils turn to p. 150 and read the text. Write the word *ancestors* on the chalkboard. Ask pupils if they know from what countries their ancestors came. Define *ancestor* as a relative or family member who lived a long time ago. As each place is mentioned, have pupils locate the place on a globe or world map.

8. Picture Reading. Have pupils look at the pictures on pp. 148–151. Point out that they are pictures of Americans who live in communities in the United States. Most American communities are made up of people of different cultural backgrounds.

Communities Celebrate Holidays

CHAPTER 6

COMMUNITIES CELEBRATE HOLIDAYS

Dear Parent,

Your child is starting the last chapter in our social studies textbook. This chapter is called "Communities Celebrate Holidays."

Children are aware that various holidays and special days occur during the year. In this chapter your child will learn why these days are important and the ways in which people celebrate them.

Many of the holidays in this chapter honor people and events that have helped to make our country great. If you have books or know stories about some of the people or events, you might want to discuss them with your child. If your family celebrates these holidays in a particular way or if you have pictures taken at a parade or celebration, share these experiences with your child.

Thank you for your interest and support.

Sincerely,

CHAPTER 6 PAGES 156–179

COMMUNITIES CELEBRATE HOLIDAYS

THEME

Holidays are celebrated to honor certain people or events.

OVERVIEW

All children have a natural interest in the festivities centered around holidays. In this chapter, pupils will learn the meaning of some holidays and the ways in which they are celebrated. Pupils will learn about the social and historical significance of people and events associated with the holidays.

BULLETIN–BOARD DISPLAY

Make a bulletin-board display covering each of the holidays that will be taught in this chapter.

If the lessons in this chapter are taught at the time when the holidays occur, a bul-letin board should be made pertaining to each lesson.

GETTING STARTED

Before starting the first lesson in this chapter, introduce pupils to a calendar. In chronological order write the months of the year on the chalkboard. Help pupils read and pronounce the names of the months. Display a large calendar showing the months. Explain that a calendar is divided into 12 parts. Each part is a month. The months are divided into weeks, and weeks are divided into days. Have pupils practice saying the days of the week and the months of the year. To test pupils' understanding of a calendar, ask questions like the following.

a. *What is the first month of the year?*

b. *Which two months begin with the letter M? With A?*

c. *How many months are in a year?*

d. *Which month comes after January? After July?*

e. *How many days are in a week?*

f. *Does each month have the same number of days?*

GOALS
1. To understand that a birthday is a special day that everyone has. 2. To tell the date of their own birthday. 3. To name the ways families celebrate birthdays.

READING VOCABULARY
birthday

TEACHING SUGGESTIONS
1. **Vocabulary Development.** Write the word *birthday* on the chalkboard. Ask pupils to think of as many words as possible associated with a birthday. (*Cake, happy, gift, party, surprise, candles, cards*)

Have pupils turn to pp. 158–159 and read the text silently. Call on individual pupils to read one or two sentences aloud.

2. **Picture Reading.** Have pupils study the picture on p. 158 and pose the following questions:

a. *How do the children in the picture feel?* (Happy)

b. *Why are they happy?*

c. *What is going on in the picture?* (A birthday party)

Ask pupils who have had or who have attended a birthday party to tell the class about it. Explain that all people do not have birthday parties. People celebrate in different ways. Some families do things such as go to a movie, to the zoo, or out to dinner. Ask pupils to name other things families might do on birthdays.

3. **Writing.** Have the class copy the following sentences and fill in the blanks:

a. *My birthday is in __.*

b. *I will be __ years old.*

c. *On my birthday I would like to __.* Have pupils write a few sentences telling what they would like to do on their birthdays.

4. **Music.** Teach the class to sing the "Birthday Song" from *Silver Burdett Music, Early Childhood,* 1981 ed.

5. **Art.** Have pupils draw a picture of something they would like to have as a birthday gift.

6. **Group Work.** Help pupils plan a birthday party for the class. This will give pupils whose birthdays fall in the summer months a chance to celebrate them with their school friends.

Pick a date for the party. Divide the class into small groups. Assign each group a special task. For example, one group could be in charge of decorations, another group could plan the menu, and another group could make a card for each child, and so on. You might want parents to participate by donating cupcakes and candles and by providing soft drinks or fruit juice.

If possible takes pictures of the party and display them on the bulletin board.

7. **Research.** Distribute magazines or catalogs and have pupils find pictures of things they would like to give family members as birthday gifts. Tell pupils that they have $10.00 to spend and that they have to stay within that amount. This activity will help reinforce the concept of making choices.

GOALS
1. To tell why Columbus Day is celebrated. 2. To tell when Columbus Day is celebrated.

READING VOCABULARY
Christopher Columbus

ORAL VOCABULARY
holiday

TEACHING SUGGESTIONS
● 1. **Reading a Poem.** Ask the class to silently read the poem on p. 156. Explain that families celebrate special days and holidays. To help pupils understand the difference between a holiday and a special

day, tell them that a holiday is a day on which some schools, banks, and businesses are closed. Labor Day and Thanksgiving are examples of holidays. On special days, such as Valentine's Day and May Day, schools, banks, and businesses are open.

Read the poem aloud while pupils study the picture. Ask the following questions:

a. *What statue is shown in the picture?* (Statue of Liberty)

b. *Why do you think there are fireworks?* (Accept all reasonable answers.)

c. *What holiday is being celebrated?* (Independence Day)

d. *Have you ever seen a band marching down a street?*

e. *What holiday was being celebrated?*

f. *What holidays does your family celebrate?*

g. *Is your birthday a special day or a holiday?* (Special day)

You may wish to have pupils who have difficulty grasping concepts to find pictures of major holidays with which they are familiar.

2. Discussion. Ask pupils to tell what they know about Christopher Columbus. Tell pupils that holidays usually honor important people or events. Christopher Columbus was an important person. Long ago, he left Spain to look for new land. Ask pupils if they remember what people who look for new lands are called (explorers). Mention that Columbus reached America on October 12, 1492. Have pupils tell how their community celebrates Columbus Day.

3. Using a Globe. Display a classroom globe. Call on pupils to find Spain on the globe. Point out that Spain is a country across an ocean from America. Ask: *What ocean did Columbus cross to reach America?*

4. Reading for Information. Have pupils read the text on pp. 160–161 silently. Then call on pupils to read aloud the sentences that answer the following questions:

a. *What did Columbus tell about when he returned to his home?* (About the land he had found)

b. *Where did Columbus go when he left his home?* (Sailed across the ocean)

c. *When do we celebrate Columbus Day?* (Second Monday in October)

d. *What things are named for Columbus?* (Towns, cities)

5. Picture Reading. Focus pupils' attention to the picture on p. 160. Explain that this is a painting of Columbus. It shows him as a young man.

Tell the class to look at the picture at the top of the next page. Ask: *How did Columbus get to America?* Point out that the picture shows the three ships Columbus and his crew sailed in. Use the annotation to help pupils pronounce the names of the ships.

Focus pupils' attention on the pictures at the bottom of the page and have pupils tell what they see.

● **6. Research.** Tell pupils that one way we remember important people is by naming things in their honor. Ask if they know of a city, state, river, school, or street named after Christopher Columbus.

Display a large map of the United States. Help pupils find such places as Columbus, Ohio; Columbus, Indiana; Columbus, Georgia; and the Columbia River.

You may wish to have pupils who require a challenge to research and write a short story on one of the things named for Columbus.

7. Story Hour. Read the story *Let's Find Out About Christopher Columbus* by Martha and Charles Shapp.

LESSON 3   PAGES 162–163

GOALS

1. To understand the meaning of Veterans Day. **2.** To tell when Veterans Day is celebrated.

READING VOCABULARY
Veterans Day

ORAL VOCABULARY
military, army, navy, marine

TEACHING SUGGESTIONS
1. Picture Reading/Vocabulary. Have pupils look at the picture on p. 162. Write the word *military* on the chalkboard. Ask pupils if they know what the word means. Help pupils define *military* as "armed forces" and name the army, the navy and the marines as branches of the military.

Help pupils understand that the purpose of our armed forces is to protect our nation and keep us free.

As pupils study the picture ask the following questions:
a. *What kind of clothes are the people wearing?* (Uniforms)
b. *Why are they saluting?* (Uniformed military people are supposed to salute the flag when repeating the Pledge of Allegiance.)
c. *How do you salute the flag?* (By standing and facing the flag with the right hand over the heart)
2. Reading. Read pp. 162–163 with the class. Write the words *veterans* and *Veterans Day* on the chalkboard. Define *veterans* as "former members of the armed forces."
3. Reading for Information. Have pupils read the text on pp. 162–163 silently. Call on pupils to read aloud the sentences that answer the following questions:
a. *Who are veterans?*
b. *When is Veterans Day celebrated?*
c. *How do some towns and cities celebrate Veterans Day?*
d. *What do veterans do on Veterans Day?*
4. Creative Writing. Write the following sentence on the chalkboard: "I am proud of my country." Have each pupil copy the sentence and compose a pledge of two or three sentences to recite after the Pledge of Allegiance.

5. Picture Reading. Have pupils look at the picture at the top of p. 163 and tell what they see. Explain the flags are an important part of a Veterans Day parade.

Focus attention on the picture at the bottom of the page. Point out that the people in this picture are veterans. They once served in the armed forces.
6. Art. Have the class make Veterans Day banners. Give each pupil a piece of heavy cardboard cut out in the shape of a banner. Have pupils decorate and color their banners. Use a dowel or piece of heavy cardboard for the staff of the banner. To make a hanging banner, simply attach a piece of string to the banner with pieces of masking tape.
7. Creative Drama. Help the class put on a short play or skit about Veterans Day. Sing patriotic songs and have pupils march around the classroom waving their banners.

LESSON 4 PAGES 164–165

GOALS
1. To understand the significance of Thanksgiving. **2.** To tell how the first Thanksgiving was celebrated. **3.** To compare the first Thanksgiving Day celebration with present day celebrations.

READING VOCABULARY
Thanksgiving Day

TEACHING SUGGESTIONS
1. Story Hour. Read one of the following stories to the class: *Let's Find Out About Thanksgiving* by Martha and Charles Shapp or *The Thanksgiving Story* by Alice Dalgliesh.
2. Picture Reading. Have pupils look at the picture on p. 164. Ask them if they know what holiday is being celebrated. Explain that the picture shows the first Thanksgiving celebration. Ask the following questions:

a. *What does Thanksgiving mean?*
b. *Who are the people in the picture?* (Pilgrims and Indians)
c. *What were some of the foods served at the first Thanksgiving?* (Turkey, ham, fish, squash, pumpkins, and so forth)
3. Reading. Call on pupils to read the text on p. 164 aloud. Discuss why the Indians were invited to the Thanksgiving celebration. You might want to review Lesson 6 of Chapter 5.
4. Picture Reading. Have pupils study the picture at the top of p. 165. Call on pupils to tell what they see. Ask:
a. *What are the people in this picture doing?*
b. *How is this Thanksgiving celebration like the first one?*
c. *What kinds of foods are served?*
d. *What are some reasons why families today are thankful?*

Have pupils compare the two Thanksgiving Day dinners.

Focus attention on the bottom picture. Ask pupils to tell what they see. Explain that many towns and cities have a parade on Thanksgiving. Have pupils tell about Thanksgiving Day parades they have been to or seen on television.
5. Reading. Call on pupils to read the text on p. 165. Have the class take turns telling one thing for which they are thankful.
6. Art. Help the class make a mural of the first Thanksgiving Day celebration.
7. Art. Have pupils create a make-believe Thanksgiving meal. Distribute construction paper and have pupils draw and color different foods eaten on Thanksgiving.
8. Story Writing. Have pupils write a short story about the first Thanksgiving.

LESSON 5   PAGES 166–167

GOALS

1. To understand that Martin Luther King, Jr., was a great leader. **2.** To find King's birthday on a calendar.

READING VOCABULARY
Martin Luther King, Jr.

ORAL VOCABULARY
civil rights

TEACHING SUGGESTIONS
1. Picture Reading/Vocabulary Development. Have pupils turn to p. 166 and identify the person shown. Begin a discussion by asking pupils what they know about King. Write the word *civil rights* on the chalkboard. Explain that *civil rights* are "those rights guaranteed all American citizens." Martin Luther King, Jr., was a civil-rights leader.
2. Story Hour. Read one of the following books to the class: *Martin Luther King, Jr.: A Picture Story* by Margaret Boone Jones, *Martin Luther King, Jr.: A Special Bravery* by Johanna Johnston, or *The Picture Life of Martin Luther King, Jr.* by Margaret B. Young.
3. Reading. Help the class read the text on pp. 166–167. Ask the following questions:
a. *When was King born?*
b. *What did he dream of?*
c. *When do we remember Martin Luther King, Jr.?*
4. Using a Calendar. Display a calendar for the month of January. Call on pupils to find King's birthday.
5. Story Writing. Help pupils write and illustrate stories about significant events in the life of King. Use such things as the nonviolent marches, bus boycotts, the Nobel Peace Prize, and his Washington speech.
6. Picture Reading. Have pupils study the picture on p. 167 and tell what they see. Point out that each year on King's birthday many towns and cities have a parade in his honor.

LESSON 6   PAGES 168–169

GOALS

1. To understand that Abraham Lincoln

was a great leader. **2.** To tell when Lincoln's birthday is celebrated. **3.** To understand that Lincoln was the 16th president of our country.

READING VOCABULARY
Abraham Lincoln

ORAL VOCABULARY
pioneers, lawyer

TEACHING SUGGESTIONS
1. Picture Reading. Have the class turn to p. 168 and study the picture at the top left. Ask pupils if they can identify the person shown. Call on volunteers to tell what they know about Abraham Lincoln.

Tell the class the following story:

Abraham Lincoln was born on a farm in Kentucky in 1809. At that time Kentucky was a wilderness. Lincoln and his family lived in a log cabin. The cabin was small with just one room and one window.

Lincoln's family were pioneers. Pioneers are people who move to a new place and help to start a settlement. Life was hard for the pioneers. They had to grow all their own food and make everything they needed.

When Lincoln was young his family moved to another farm in Indiana. Lincoln could not attend school often because there were few teachers and he had to help on the farm. Still Lincoln learned to read and write. After working on the farm all day, he would read by candlelight or by the light of the fireplace. He used charcoal and a pen made from a turkey feather to write.

When Lincoln grew up, he had many jobs. But most of all he wanted to be a lawyer. A lawyer is a person who has studied the laws of a country.

Lincoln moved to Illinois, where he practiced law. In 1861 Lincoln became the 16th President of the United States.

2. Reading. Have pupils turn to pp. 168–169 and read the text. Display a current calendar for February. Call on pupils to find Lincoln's birthday on the calendar and name the day it comes on. Help the class figure out how old Lincoln would be on his birthday by subtracting 1809 from the current year.

3. Discussion. Start a discussion with the following:
a. *In what state was Lincoln born?* (Kentucky)
b. *What is a wilderness?*
c. *What is a log cabin?*
d. *Why do you think Lincoln went to school for only a few years?*
e. *Why did he have to teach himself to read?*
f. *Who taught you to read?*
g. *In what ways was Lincoln's life like the early colonists'?*

At this point you might want to review the words *wilderness* and *log cabin* from Chapter 5.

4. Using a Map. Display a large map of the United States. Call on pupils to find Kentucky, Indiana, and Illinois on the map.

5. Picture Reading. Have the class look at the picture at the bottom of p. 168. Explain that the picture shows Lincoln as a boy studying by the light of the fireplace. Focus attention on the picture on the right of p. 168. Point out that Lincoln worked at many jobs. Here he is splitting rail logs.

Have pupils look at the picture on p. 169. Ask if they know what the picture shows. Point out that this statue is in the Lincoln Memorial in Washington, D.C.

6. Story Hour. Read to the class the story *Let's Find Out About Abraham Lincoln* by Martha and Charles Shapp.

7. Letter Writing. Divide the class into two groups. Have one group write letters to Lincoln asking about his home, friends, school, and family. Have the other group pretend to be Abraham Lincoln and answer the letters.

GOALS

1. To understand that George Washington was the first President of our country. **2.** To find Virginia and Washington, D.C., on a Unted States map.

READING VOCABULARY

George Washington

ORAL VOCABULARY

Mount Vernon

TEACHING SUGGESTIONS

1. Reading. Have pupils turn to p. 170 and read the text. Ask pupils to tell what they know about George Washington. Read the following story to the class:

George Washington was born on February 22, 1732. Washington lived with his family on a large farm in Virginia. Young George loved games, swimming, and fishing. He wanted to be outdoors as much as he could. George was especially fond of horses. He practiced riding almost every day. But George didn't spend all his time playing; he also went to school. George was a good student. His favorite subject was arithmetic.

When George was a young man, our country fought a war. George Washington was chosen to lead the army. Everyone called him General Washington. After the war George was chosen to be President. He was proud that the people of America chose him to be their very first President.

2. Using a Map. Display a map of the United States. Call on volunteers to find Virginia and Washington, D.C., on the map.

3. Discussion. Tell the class that many things are named for George Washington. List the following examples on the chalkboard—the state of Washington, George Washington Bridge, Washington Monument. Discuss these things with the class.

4. Research. Distribute travel magazines and have pupils find pictures of things named after Washington.

5. Reading/Picture Reading. Have pupils read the text on p. 171 silently as you read aloud. Ask the following questions:

a. *Which person shown in the picture is George Washington?*

b. *Who are the other people?* (Soldiers)

Direct pupils' attention to the bottom picture. Use the annotation to explain the picture.

6. Using a Calendar. Display a calendar for the current year. Have pupils find when Washington's birthday will be celebrated.

7. Story Hour. Read one of the following books to the class: *Washington's Birthday* by Clyde Robert Bulla or *A Man Named Washington* by Gertrude Norman.

GOALS

1. To understand the purpose of Memorial Day. **2.** To tell when Memorial Day is celebrated. **3.** To make a chart of holidays.

READING VOCABULARY

Memorial Day

ORAL VOCABULARY

wreath, Decoration Day

TEACHING SUGGESTIONS

1. Discussion. Write the words *Memorial Day* on the chalkboard. Start a discussion by saying, *The purpose of Memorial Day was to honor those who died in the Civil War. Later Memorial Day was celebrated to honor all who lost their life in wars. Today we honor not only those who died in wars but also dead family members and friends.*

2. Reading/Vocabulary Development. Have pupils turn to p. 172 and silently read the text as you read it aloud. Ask pupils if they know what the words *services* and *programs* mean. Write the words on the chalkboard.

3. Picture Reading. Have pupils study the pictures on pp. 172–173. Ask the following questions:

a. *What symbol of our country is shown in these pictures?* (The flag)

b. *What are the children in the pictures doing?* (Scouts take part in services and programs and also march in Memorial Day parades.)

Explain that many people place wreaths near tombs and monuments. For this reason Memorial Day is also know as Decoration Day. Have pupils find the wreath in the picture on p. 172.

4. Using a Calendar. Display a large calendar for the month of May. Before having pupils tell when Memorial Day is celebrated, point out that in some parts of our country Memorial Day is celebrated on the last Monday and in some other places it is celebrated on the last Friday. Help pupils find out when Memorial Day is celebrated in their community.

• **5. Making a Chart.** Distribute construction paper and have pupils each make a chart titled "Holidays of the Year." List the 12 months in a vertical column, and have pupils fill in the holidays discussed in this chapter beside the month in which the holiday is celebrated.

You may wish to have pupils who require a challenge research other holidays to add to their chart.

LESSON 9   PAGES 174–175

GOALS

1. To understand that Independence Day is our country's birthday. **2.** To tell when Independence Day is celebrated. **3.** To find England on a globe.

READING VOCABULARY
Independence Day

ORAL VOCABULARY
fife

TEACHING SUGGESTIONS

1. Reading. Write the words *Independence Day* on the chalkboard. Read the text on p. 174 aloud as pupils read along silently. Call on pupils to read aloud the sentences that answer the following questions:

a. *How many states did our country have long ago?* (Thirteen)

b. *Who made many of the laws and rules that the people in America had to follow long ago?* (The king)

c. *Where did the king live?* (England)

d. *What did England and America do?* (Fought a war)

e. *Who won the war?* (Americans)

2. Using a Globe. Display a classroom globe. Help pupils locate England, the Atlantic Ocean, and the land that made up the thirteen states in America.

3. Picture Reading. Focus pupils' attention on the picture on p. 174. Ask them to describe what they see. Write the word *fife* on the chalkboard. Explain that a fife is a musical instrument. In this picture the fife player and two drummers are leading American troops into battle in the War for Independence.

4. Reading. Have pupils turn to p. 175 and call on volunteers to read the text aloud. Ask the following questions:

a. *How many states does our country have today?* (Fifty)

b. *What is our country's symbol?* (The flag)

c. *When is Independence Day celebrated?*

5. Story Hour. Read to the class *Fourth of July* by Charles Grasser.

6/CHAPTER REVIEW   PAGE 176–177

Answers to Review Questions

1. Birthday
2. October
3. George Washington
4. Independence Day; the Fourth of July
5. Fifty
6. Each state in the United States
7. Thirteen
8. The first thirteen states or colonies